796·72

THE MONACO GRAND PRIX

ALEX ROLLO

First published 1987

ISBN 0 7110 1748 4

© Alex Rollo 1987

Published by Ian Allan Ltd., Shepperton,
Surrey.

Produced by Palatine Hill, Yeovil,
Somerset.

Book design by Doug Kenyon.

CONTENTS

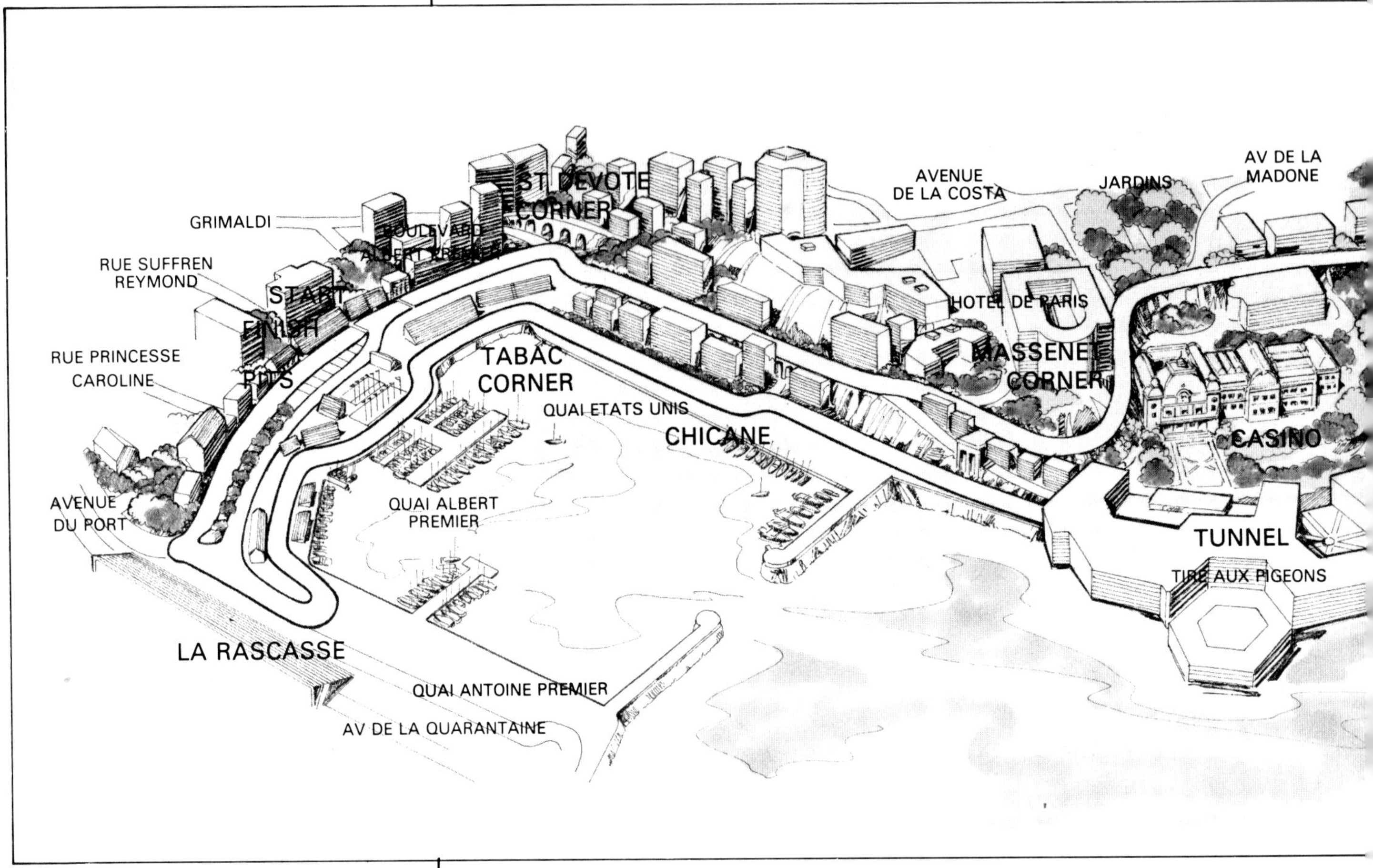

GRIMALDI

RUE SUFFREN
REYMOND

RUE PRINCESSE
CAROLINE

ST DEVOTE
CORNER

BOULEVARD
ALBERT PREMIER

START
FINISH
PITS

AVENUE
DE LA COSTA

JARDINS

AV DE LA
MADONE

HOTEL DE PARIS

MASSENET
CORNER

TABAC
CORNER

QUAI ETATS UNIS

CHICANE

CASINO

AVENUE
DU PORT

QUAI ALBERT
PREMIER

TUNNEL

TIRE AUX PIGEONS

LA RASCASSE

QUAI ANTOINE PREMIER

AV DE LA QUARANTAINE

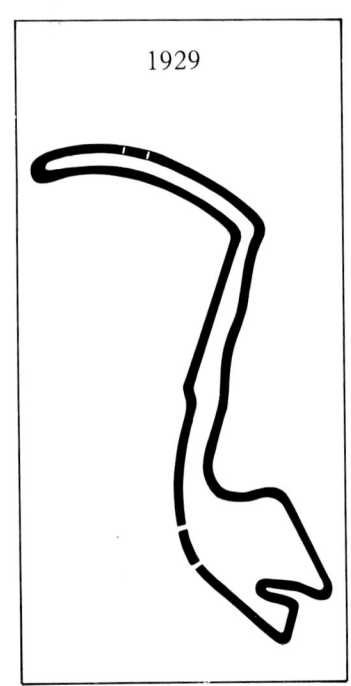

1929

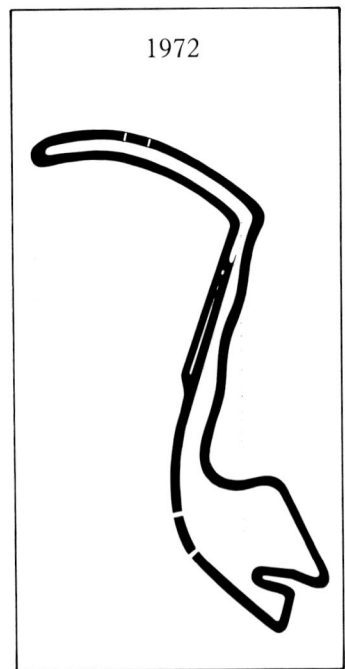

1972

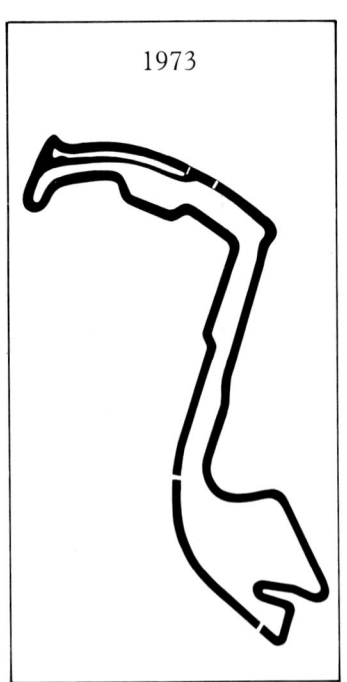

1973

INTRODUCTION

Judge the reaction if it was proposed to race 500 b.h.p. Formula One racing cars around the streets of your home town. For nearly a week it would be necessary to close the shopping centre to normal traffic for several hours each day. The circuit would be bordered by crash barriers, but there would probably be a number of crashes, possibly involving personal injury. The noise would be deafening and would undoubtedly be heard within a radius of five miles. The motor racing fan would see probably the slowest race on the calendar, with limited visibility of the circuit. Only twenty cars would be allowed to start and of these probably only half of them at best would finish.

I suggest that any such proposal would be treated with a good deal of derision in most towns with which we are familiar. And yet, the above is a thumbnail sketch of one of the world's greatest Grand Prix races.

The Monaco Grand Prix has been held in such circumstances since its inception in 1929 and is today probably one of the best known motor races in existence. It is a test of driver and engineering skill, a sporting event, and a social event, at one and the same time.

The bulk of this book concentrates on the modern era of the race, therefore I have chosen to start my detailed race analysis from 1961 and the introduction of the 1½-litre formula to Formula One, and with the almost universal adoption of the rear-engine design of car.

It is not difficult to be enthusiastic about the Monaco Grand Prix. On a league table of Grand Prix motor racing few would place it outside of the top three, and many would not hesitate to nominate the race as the world's premier motoring test. What makes a great Grand Prix?

Primarily, I believe, the function of motor racing is not just to excite a crowd, or to make the organisers lots of money. The function of racing must be to prove the quality of the cars, and the skills of the drivers, and in the process, develop the standards of both. The French term 'Grande Epreuve' is, to my mind, a better title than Grand Prix, particularly in the case of Monaco, which as a test of car and driver stands supreme. In a race consisting of 100 laps of ten corners per lap, (including three bottom gear hairpin bends), over thirty gear shifts per lap, constant braking and fierce acceleration, the strain on car transmission, suspension, tyres and brakes is supreme.

MONACO GRAND PRIX ROLL OF HONOUR

1929	Williams *(Bugatti)*
	Bouriano *(Bugatti)*
	Caracciola *(Mercedes-Benz)*
1930	Dreyfus *(Bugatti)*
	Chiron *(Bugatti)*
	Bouriat *(Bugatti)*
1931	Chiron *(Bugatti)*
	Fagiola *(Maserati)*
	Varzi *(Bugatti)*
1932	Nuvolari *(Alfa Romeo)*
	Caracciola *(Alfa Romeo)*
	Fagioli *(Maserati)*
1933	Varzi *(Bugatti)*
	Borzacchini *(Alfa Romeo)*
	Dreyfus *(Bugatti)*
1934	Moll *(Alfa Romeo)*
	Chiron *(Alfa Romeo)*
	Dreyfus *(Bugatti)*
1935	Fagioli *(Mercedes Benz)*
	Dreyfus *(Alfa Romeo)*
	Brivio *(Alfa Romeo)*
1936	Caracciola *(Mercedes Benz)*
	Varzi *(Auto Union)*
	Stuck *(Auto Union)*
1937	von Brauchitsch *(Mercedes Benz)*
	Caracciola *(Mercedes Benz)*
	Kautz *(Mercedes Benz)*
1948	Farina *(Maserati)*
	Chiron *(Talbot)*
	de Graffenried *(Maserati)*
1950	Fangio *(Alfa Romeo)*
	Ascari *(Ferrari)*
	Chiron *(Maserati)*
1952	Marzotto *(Ferrari)*
	Castellotti *(Ferrari)*
	Slagnoti/Biondetti *(Ferrari)*
1955	Trintignant *(Ferrari)*
	Castellotti *(Lancia)*
	Behra/Perdisa *(Maserati)*
1956	Moss *(Maserati)*
	Collins/Fangio *(Ferrari)*
	Behra *(Maserati)*
1957	Fangio *(Maserati)*
	Brooks *(Vanwall)*
	Gregory *(Maserati)*
1958	Trintignant *(Cooper-Climax)*
	Musso *(Ferrari)*
	Collins *(Ferrari)*
1959	Brabham *(Cooper-Climax)*
	Brooks *(Ferrari)*
	Trintignant *(Cooper-Climax)*
1960	Moss *(Lotus-Climax)*
	McLaren *(Cooper-Climax)*
	P. Hill *(Ferrari)*
1961	Moss *(Lotus-Climax)*
	Ginther *(Ferrari)*
	P. Hill *(Ferrari)*
1962	McLaren *(Cooper-Climax)*
	P. Hill *(Ferrari)*
	Bandini *(Ferrari)*
1963	G. Hill *(B.R.M.)*
	Ginther *(B.R.M.)*
	McLaren *(Cooper-Climax)*

5

1964	G. Hill *(B.R.M.)*	
	Ginther *(B.R.M.)*	
	Arundell *(Lotus-Climax)*	
1965	G. Hill *(B.R.M.)*	
	Bandini *(Ferrari)*	
	Stewart *(B.R.M.)*	
1966	Stewart *(B.R.M.)*	
	Bandini *(Ferrari)*	
	G. Hill *(B.R.M.)*	
1967	Hulme *(Brabham)*	
	G. Hill *(Lotus)*	
	Amon *(Ferrari)*	
1968	G. Hill *(Lotus)*	
	Attwood *(B.R.M.)*	
	Bianchi *(Cooper)*	
1969	G. Hill *(Lotus)*	
	Courage *(Brabham)*	
	Siffert *(Lotus)*	
1970	Rindt *(Lotus)*	
	Brabham *(Brabham)*	
	Pescarolo *(Matra-Simca)*	
1971	Stewart *(Tyrrell)*	
	Peterson *(March)*	
	Ickx *(Ferrari)*	
1972	Beltoise *(B.R.M.)*	
	Ickx *(Ferrari)*	
	Fittipaldi *(Lotus)*	
1973	Stewart *(Tyrrell)*	
	Fittipaldi *(Lotus)*	
	Peterson *(Lotus)*	
1974	Peterson *(Lotus)*	
	Scheckter *(Tyrrell)*	
	Jarier *(Shadow)*	
1975	Lauda *(Ferrari)*	
	Fittipaldi *(McLaren)*	
	Pace *(Brabham)*	
1976	Lauda *(Ferrari)*	
	Scheckter *(Tyrrell)*	
	Depailler *(Tyrrell)*	
1977	Scheckter *(Wolf)*	
	Lauda *(Ferrari)*	
	Reutemann *(Ferrari)*	
1978	Depailler *(Tyrrell)*	
	Lauda *(Brabham)*	
	Scheckter *(Wolf)*	
1979	Scheckter *(Ferrari)*	
	Regazzoni *(Williams)*	
	Reutemann *(Lotus)*	
1980	Reutemann *(Williams)*	
	Lafitte *(Ligier)*	
	Piquet *(Brabham)*	
1981	Villeneuve *(Ferrari)*	
	Jones *(Williams)*	
	Lafitte *(Talbot)*	
1982	Patrese *(Brabham)*	
	Pironi *(Ferrari)*	
	de Cesaris *(Alfa Romeo)*	
1983	Rosberg *(Williams)*	
	Piquet *(Brabham)*	
	Prost *(Renault)*	
1984	Prost *(McLaren)*	
	Senna *(Toleman)*	
	Bellof *(Tyrrell)*	
1985	Prost *(McLaren)*	
	Alboreto *(Ferrari)*	
	de Angelis *(Lotus)*	
1986	Prost *(McLaren)*	
	Rosberg *(McLaren)*	
	Senna *(Lotus)*	

The course itself is completely unforgiving, with its Armco fencing, high kerb stones and very few run-off areas. One minor driver error can completely disable a car. Therefore, driver concentration and performance must be perfect from start to finish, in conditions that are frequently very hot, and always very tiring.

Some would argue that there is a lack of quality racing at Monaco because of its limited overtaking areas, and yet every year the race provides more than its share of drama and excitement, and always attracts massive crowds of supporters. Remember Jack Brabham's last lap spin which allowed Rindt through to win in 1970?

Few races are held in more dramatic surroundings than Monaco. The town provides the photographer's dream background, while the noise echoing off the buildings is shattering and unforgettable. A harbour full of the world's finest yachts, and overlooked by the pink palace; the town packed with thousands of excited fans; all contribute to produce an atmosphere unique only to Monaco.

The race was first run in 1929 and has been run 44 times. Its list of winners includes the great drivers of motor racing. Few of them would have considered their careers completely successful without their name appearing at least once on the Monaco roll of honour. There is no doubt that a win here enhances a driver's status more than any other race, and perhaps therein lies the ultimate accolade - the world's greatest motor race!

The object of this book is to bring the history of the Monaco Grand Prix up to date, but I will not attempt to disguise or excuse my enthusiasm for the event, and I hope my readers will find themselves infected by the disease, which, in my case at least, is incurable!

The feature of any book on Monaco must be the photographs. The photographs of David Phipps and his team are well known to motoring enthusiasts throughout the world. He has been a regular visitor to the Monaco Grand Prix for nearly 30 years and still enjoys every minute spent there.

I am also very grateful to the National Motor Museum at Beaulieu who dug into their extensive archives to find all of the early photographs included.

Footnote
The source of reference for the results panels in this book was *Motorsport,* to whom we are indebted for their painstaking recording of detail over so many years.

6

The Principality of Monaco consists of a series of connected towns: Monaco-Ville, overlooking the port; Fontvielle, the industrial area; La Condamine, the commercial centre; and Monte Carlo. Monaco is a fashionable resort renowned for its royal family, its oceanographical museum, its gambling casino, the Monte Carlo Rally and the Monaco Grand Prix motor race.

Tourism is the chief source of income for the Monagasques, and therefore the House of Grimaldi and the government have always been conscious of the need to attract visitors to the area, particularly those with money to spend. The average Monagasque has never been shy in accepting a franc - or any other currency for that matter!

It was in 1928 that the newly formed Automobile Club de Monaco applied through its President, Anthony Noghes, for admission to the International Association of Recognised Automobile Clubs (later to become F.I.F.A.). Noghes encountered some resistance from the I.A.R.A.C. officials, who expressed serious doubts about the ability of the A.C.M. to meet the necessary racing standards of the day within the confined area of Monaco. In some desperation, Noghes announced his intention to run an international Grand Prix race through the streets of the town the following year. The event, at that time, was only a vague possibility since the project did not have the approval of the local authorities, let alone the support of the Grimaldi family! Noghes had gambled and then had to set about making good his boast.

Fortunately for Noghes, the idea was greeted with enthusiasm by the royal family, who were ever open to proposals which might be beneficial to the Principality. With the support of H.S.H. Prince Peter, the Automobile Club soon had the full co-operation of the public

The start of the first Monaco Grand Prix in 1929. The front row of the starting grid comprised a full set of Bugattis.

services. Noghes himself selected what he felt was the only possible circuit - starting at the port, along the quay via Boulevard Albert Premier, up the hill of Monte Carlo and through the Place du Casino, down the hill to the railway station, and from the station through the Tir aux Pigeons tunnel back to the port.

That was the original circuit. That is the circuit today. Some of the buildings have changed or disappeared, and the road has been improved, but in essence the circuit is unchanged in 57 years. 'The race of 1000 corners' - 1.97 miles per lap, 10 corners per lap, 100 laps - this was the first genuine 'round the houses' motor race. It is by nature, rather than by design, a tight, demanding course, hard on both cars and drivers.

The first race was run, on schedule, in 1929. Noghes' dream was reality. The race was a massive success and set in motion a series of motor races unrivalled for spectacle, drama or excitement.

The roll of honour of the Monaco Grand Prix is a list of the great racing drivers and the great racing cars of their day. It can safely be said that no 'ordinary' driver ever won there. Very few of the great champions did not win there (Jim Clarke being a rare exception). Nuvolari, Varzi, Caracciola, Farina, Fangio, Trintignant Moss,

Graham Hill, Stewart, Lauda, Rosberg, Prost - all won there while at their peak. The best car did not always win, however, but here we have the influence of the human element. The Moss win in an outdated Lotus in 1961 is the classic example of driver skill overcoming the inferior performance of an old, if very good car. This, of course, adds to the fascination of Monaco.

The first race had 16 starters, Bugatti, Maserati, Delage, Alfa Romeo, Licorne, every car supercharged (so with today's grid of all turbocharged cars, racing could be said to have come the full circle). The formula was quite open compared with today's strictly enforced parameters. On the grid were to be found 1.5-litre Bugattis, 1.75-litre Alfa Romeos, 2.0-litre Maseratis, and a sole 7.1-litre SSK Mercedes Benz.

It is interesting that the use of practice times to determine position on the starting grid, was introduced at Monaco in the 1933 race. Previously position was determined by lot. A good grid position has always been vital at Monaco - perhaps more important than any other race, because of the nature of the course and the difficulties in overtaking. This, to the enthusiast, always adds to the interest because practice becomes a race in itself, rather than just a mechanical trial of the cars.

The first winner of the Monaco Grand Prix in 1929 was Williams in a Bugatti, seen here with his mechanic - almost in the passenger seat!

Left
Gasworks Hairpin 1929. The harbour full of great steam yachts.

9

Louis Chiron leads Williams around
the Gasworks Hairpin in 1930 - both in
Bugattis. Chiron later became the
Race Director for many years. Note
the tram lines!

In 1934 the 750 kg formula was introduced (cars weighed dry, without wheels). Engine capacity was unlimited but initially a capacity of between 2.5-litres and 2.9-litres was most common. However, by 1935 and the appearance of the Mercedes Benz team cars, sheer power was considered all important. The W.25s were of 3.99-litres, the sole Bugatti (Howe) was now 3.3-litres, the Alfa Romeos were bored out to 3.15-litres, and some of the Maseratis 3.7-litres. In 1936 the Mercedes were 4.74-litres, the Alfas 3.8-litres, the Maseratis 4.8-litres, and even the sole Bugatti 4.7-litres. Auto Unions appeared with the first rear-engined cars at Monaco, powered by V 16s of 6-litres. In 1937, the last race before the war and a ten year break, the grid consisted of the most powerful cars ever seen on the roads. The Mercedes Benz W.125 was of 5.66-litres capacity, and the Auto Union C-type, 6-litres. The rest could not com-

The Alfa Romeo Team took first and second in the 1934 Grand Prix.

Alfa Romeo Monoposto in 1934 in the Quai Albert Premier.

pete. The first three rows of the grid consisted of German cars and von Brauchitsch won from Caracciola and Kautz - all in Mercedes. The race average was 3.1 m.p.h. faster than the existing lap record, and Caracciola's new lap record was to stand for 18 years! Brute force was the order of the day - perhaps significant at that time!

After the war, naturally motor racing was low on the world's list of priorities and it was not until 1948 that the 10th Monaco Grand Prix was to take place. The new racing formula was 1.5-litres supercharged or 4.5-litres unsupercharged. The new line up consisted of Maseratis, Simca-Gordinis, Talbots, ERAs and, significantly, a Ferrari. Farina won in the Maserati at 59.74 m.p.h. from Chiron in a Talbot, the average speed being over 3 m.p.h. down on the pre-war record.

The race was not run in 1949 but a more organised field appeared for 1950. This was to be Fangio's year and the first of the great mans' two Monaco victories. Unfortunately for the spectators the race had been spoiled by a second lap crash which eliminated 10 of the 19 car field. Fangio's Type 158 Alfa Romeo averaged 61.33 m.p.h., and he was the first man in the history of the race to lap the field.

12

Again the race missed a year in 1951 and the 1952 race was for sports cars. On the front row of the grid appeared a certain S. Moss driving a Jaguar! Stirling in fact led the race for 24 laps before being involved in another multi-car pile-up at Ste. Devote. He managed to restart but was later disqualified for receiving outside assistance. Marzotto eventually won in a Ferrari from Castellotti, also in a Ferrari.

After a three year break the single seat Grand Prix cars returned to Monaco in 1955 for the 13th running of the race. For the first time it was nominated the 'Grand Prix d'Europe', and attracted the quality field it deserved. Mercedes turned out a three car team which included the formidable combination of Moss and Fangio. It was to no avail, however, since both cars failed while in the

Castellotti in the 1955 Lancia D.50 with pannier fuel tanks between the wheels.

14

lead. Trintignant won in the Ferrari by a comfortable 20 seconds from Castellotti's Lancia.

1956 was Stirling's year and yet another Moss/Fangio battle. Now driving for Maserati and Ferrari respectively, they led the qualifiers with Fangio on pole position. Nevertheless, Moss was first into the Gasworks Hairpin and was never headed, Fangio having made a rare mistake early on, spinning his car at Ste. Devote. Even so, he made a spirited chase and worked his way up through the field to second place, before finally damaging a wheel on the Ferrari and retiring the car. He then took over the car of his team mate Collins to continue the chase, but finally had to settle for second best, six seconds behind the triumphant winner. Once again Monaco had brought the best out of two great drivers!

The lifetime ambition of Stirling Moss to be successful in a British Formula One car at last entered the realms of possibility with the emergence of the Vanwall. The marque had made its first appearance at Monaco in 1955, in the hands of Mike Hawthorne, and performed respectably before being retired while in tenth place. In 1956 it again retired, this time with overheating, (Trintignant the driver this time). However, progress was being made, and in 1957 two cars were entered - to be driven by Moss and Brooks. In practice Moss achieved third fastest, while Brooks made the second row with the fourth fastest time. The race was over 105 laps for the first time, instead of the customary 100. Moss made his

Primitive crash barriers save Lancia and Ferrari from the harbour - 1955.

usual good start and was soon leading, but on the fourth lap he was over-enthusiastic at the chicane, and his race was over. Brooks settled down to drive a steady race, deciding not to challenge the great Fangio in the Maserati, who came home comfortably for his second Monaco win. Brooks brought the Vanwall in for a well deserved second place.

1958 was Fangio's last year in Grand Prix racing, his last race being at the French Grand Prix (Reims). It was to be Mike Hawthorne's year for the championship: in a close contest with Moss, his one win and five seconds pipped Stirling's four wins. Moss was never to win the world championship, and though it is unlikely that he ever gave it a thought, under the present points system he would have won in both 1957 and 1958.

The 1958 race, the 16th Monaco Grand Prix, was a disaster for Vanwall (three cars entered, three retired), but brought the first win for a British car. Trintignant won with the Cooper-Climax at an average speed of 67.98 m.p.h., and the continental domination of the event was at last interrupted. This was only the beginning, for British cars were to win for the next sixteen years, and the British mechanical superiority in Grand Prix racing to dominate until the present day.

1959 and 1960 were the final years of the old 2.5-litre formula and the emergence of the rear-engined car. Rear engines were not new to Monaco - Auto Union in particular having placed a lot of faith and money into the format before the war. However, it took the Cooper team and the Coventry-Climax engine company to demonstrate its advantages in the modern Grand Prix car.

Brabham's win in the 1959 Monaco Grand Prix in a Cooper-Climax and the Moss win in a Lotus-Climax in 1960, clearly showed the way, with cars that were not only quick in a straight line, but fast on a 'round the houses' course. B.R.M. also produced their first rear-engined car for the 1960 race, and by 1961 the whole grid had rear-engined rear-wheel drive cars. The new way had been clearly demonstrated and a new formula had been defined, even though it had many critics. It was now up to the engineers to make the best use of the opportunity, and with the Monaco Grand Prix now well established at the beginning of the season, the future for Monaco enthusiasts was most promising.

16

Jo Bonnier in a B.R.M. leads Stirling Moss and his Lotus-Climax through the early laps of the 1960 race. Both cars were rear-engined, which was to become the format of the future.

17

Above
The first day's practice was ruled out in 1969 when wings were ruled illegal. Seen here is the B.R.M. of Oliver, in practice before the ban.

Top left
Jo Bonnier leads on the first lap - 1960.

Left inset
The 1964 winner, Graham Hill in the B.R.M. V8.

Top
Bandini (17) and his team mate Surtees drove the Ferraris to second and fourth places in 1965.

Middle right
Hulme's 1967 win was overshadowed by the death of Bandini.

Main picture
A stylish win for Graham Hill in the Lotus 49/5 - Monaco 1968. Note the adjustable front wings and the engine cover/spoiler.

Left
Jochen Rindt in the Lotus 49 coming down the hill from the tunnel. Rindt took advantage of Jack Brabham's last corner error to snatch a dramatic win.

Left

Ronnie Peterson (Lotus 72) led the early stages of the 1973 race, before mechanical problems slowed him down.

Above
Niki Lauda finally won for Ferrari in 1975. Their previous win was in 1955 -the sports car race.

Top
The 1973 winner Jackie Stewart in the Tyrrell.

Middle
Ronnie Peterson drove the Lotus to a Monaco win in 1974.

Main picture
Emerson Fittipaldi produced another-fine performance for McLaren when he took second place to Lauda - 1975.

Niki Lauda in a Ferrari 312 leads Ronnie Peterson in the March 761 by the harbour - 1976.

Above
Scheckter again, this time driving the Wolf to victory in 1977.

Top
Emerson Fittipaldi (McLaren) ahead of Ronnie Peterson (Lotus) in the early stages - 1975.

Middle
Jody Scheckter in the six wheel Tyrrell - 1976.

Above
Reutemann - Williams Cosworth V8.

Top
Scheckter leads the field to Ste. Devote after the 1979 start. It was nearly the perfect race - he held pole position and led the race from start to finish.

Middle
1980 - Reutemann (Williams) leads Laffitte (Ligier) up to Monte Carlo. Reutemann won after Pironi hit a barrier late in the race.

Patrick Depailler won his first ever Grand Prix in 1978 driving the Tyrrell.

Above
Alain Prost - third in 1983. A wrong choice of tyres probably cost him the race.

Top
Monaco 1981 - Quai Etats Unis.

Top middle
Riccardo Patrese - 1982 winner in a Brabham Cosworth V8.

Middle
Didier Pironi - Ferrari V6 t/c. Second in 1982.

Inset
The 1983 race was won by Rosberg in the Williams. His gamble on 'slick' tyres from the start paid off.

In a race shortened by bad weather Alain Prost came home a rather fortunate winner in 1984.

Above
Ayrton Senna in the Toleman came through the field to finish second.

Top
Both Renaults were eliminated in a first lap crash at Ste. Devote.

Top middle
Nigel Mansell in the Lotus led a Grand Prix for the first time ever, but soon threw his chance away when he lost control in the slippery conditions.

Middle
Alain Prost in the Marlboro McLaren.

Above
Rosberg played second fiddle to Prost in 1986, to complete a fine team performance for McLaren.

Top
Alboreto in the Ferrari was the hero of the 1985 race.

Lower top
A steady drive in 1985 gave de Angelis and Lotus third place.

Middle
A second win in a row for Prost in '85.

Inset
Alain Prost, World Champion in 1985. Took pole position, set a new lap record and dominated the 1986 race.

Below
Piquet in the second Williams and Lafitte in a Ligier. Piquet had a miserable time in 1986, with a car that never ran at its best. Lafitte started the race from the back of the grid and drove a fine race to finish sixth.

'61 A NEW ERA

A new era in Grand Prix motor racing began at the start of the 1961 Formula One season with the advent of the new 1½-litre Formula. Development of the old 2½-litre Formula was close to reaching exhaustion and many were concerned about safety, feeling that restrictions were necessary. Reducing maximum engine capacity to 1500 c.c. with a maximum weight of 450 kilogrammes (990 lbs.) gave the engineers a new problem to get their teeth into, and, in theory at least, would slow everyone down. The enthusiasts were disappointed at the decision, expecting a period of dull racing, and some drivers were even concerned that lack of power would prove dangerous. The 1961 Monaco Grand Prix surely resolved their apprehension, even if it didn't make the

ENTRIES

DRIVER	TEAM	CAR
J. Bonnier	Porsche	Porsche
D. Gurney	Porsche	Porsche
H. Herrmann	Porsche	Porsche
M. May	Seidal	Lotus-Climax
L. Bianchi	Equipe National Belge	Emeryson-Climax
O. Gendebien	Equipe National Belge	Emeryson-Climax
M. Gregory	Comaradi	Cooper-Climax
C.A.S. Brooks	B.R.M.	B.R.M.-Climax
G. Hill	B.R.M.	B.R.M.-Climax
S. Moss	Walker	Lotus-Climax
J. Surtees	Yeoman Credit	Cooper-Climax
J. Brabham	Cooper	Cooper-Climax
B. McLaren	Cooper	Cooper-Climax
J. Clark	Lotus	Lotus-Climax
I. Ireland	Lotus	Lotus-Climax
C. Allison	U.D.T.-Laystall	Lotus-Climax
H.C. Taylor	U.D.T.-Laystall	Lotus-Climax
P.R. Ginther	Ferrari	Ferrari-V6
P. Hill	Ferrari	Ferrari-V6
W. von Trips	Ferrari	Ferrari-V6
M. Trintignant	Parnell	Cooper-Climax

Above
Dan Gurney in the Porsche.

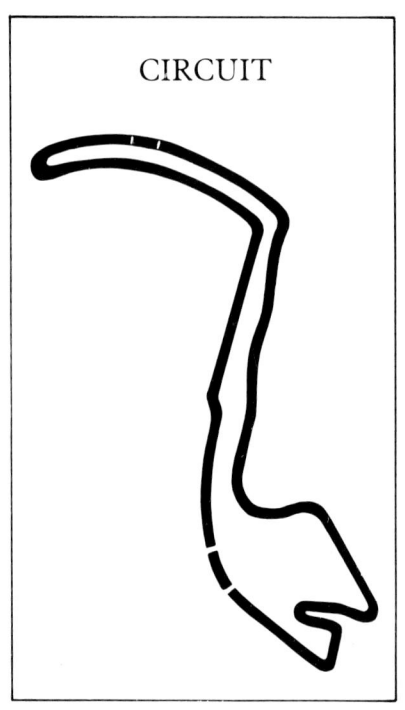

CIRCUIT

safety lobby any happier!

As a result of the effort put into opposing the new formula, development of cars in time for the opening of the season was much retarded. Of the major teams only Ferrari were really prepared. All the other teams were confined to entering modified Formula Two cars, until new engines and chassis could be prepared.

Only one Formula One race had been held prior to the 1961 Monaco Grand Prix, that being at Siracusa, where Giancarlo Baghetti in a Ferrari showed his tail to the cream of the Grand Prix drivers. Furthermore at Monaco Ferrari had a new 120-degree V6-cylinder engine ready for Ginther. The Ferrari team were rubbing their hands in anticipation. They had forgotten that man called Moss!

As usual the field was limited to 16 starters, but unlike previous years where the fastest qualifiers made

the grid, each factory team was guaranteed two places. Previous winners were also guaranteed places - these going to Moss and Trintignant, leaving only four places available for the remainder to fight over. Practice began on Thursday for all except the Porsche team of Bonnier, Gurney and Herrmann, who were still awaiting the arrival of their cars. Graham Hill and Brooks were driving for B.R.M., Brabham and McLaren for Cooper, Clark and Ireland for Lotus, Gendebien and Bianchi for Equipe National Belge, Allison and Taylor for U.D.T.-Laystall. Gregory drove the Camoradi Cooper, May the Siedal Lotus and Surtees the Yeoman Credit Cooper. Moss turned out the Walker Lotus, and Trintignant a Cooper-Maserati.

Fastest of the day was Clark in the brand new Lotus with 1 min. 39.6, immediately before wrecking the car at Ste. Devote corner. Ginther and Phil Hill recorded 1

Stirling Moss in the Walker Lotus-Climax driving to a classic win.

Left
The start at Monaco 1961. Ginther leads Clarke and Moss through Gasworks Hairpin.

STARTING GRID

28	36	20
Clark	**Ginther**	**Moss**
1 min. 39.6	1 min. 39.3	1 min. 39.1

38	18
P. Hill	**G. Hill**
1 min. 39.8	1 min. 39.6

16	26	40
Brooks	**McLaren**	**von Trips**
1 min. 40.1	1 min. 39.8	1 min. 39.8

4	2
Gurney	**Bonnier**
1 min. 40.6	1 min. 40.3

8	6	22
May	**Herrmann**	**Surtees**
1 min. 42.0	1 min. 41.1	1 min. 41.1

42	32
Trintignant	**Allison**
1 min. 42.4	1 min. 42.3

24
Brabham
1 min. 44.0

Phil Hill, the great American driver, swings the beautiful Ferrari V6 through Station Hairpin.

min. 41, each with von Trips close behind on 1 min. 41.7. The previous year's winner Stirling Moss recorded 1 min. 41.1, Innes Ireland 1 min. 41.5 and Graham Hill 1 min. 42.8.

An early start on the Friday brought about the appearance of the Porsche team and very soon all three recorded times in the low 1 min. 40s, Bonnier fastest in 1 min. 41.9. Almost everyone showed good improvement with Ginther leading so far on 1 min. 39.3.

Saturday's final thrash was held in perfect conditions, without Clark, whose Lotus was still being reassembled, and Brabham who was qualifying at Indianapolis. Ireland, who had not been happy with the Lotus gear shift throughout practice, missed a change in the tunnel and wrote off his car, putting himself into hospital in the process. The four available qualifying places were claimed by Ginther, Surtees, Herrmann and May, with Allison creeping in as replacement for Ireland.

Sunday, May 14th and there was perfect weather for the race - warm and dry with clouds obscuring the sun. The start at 2.45 p.m. was perfect with Ginther stealing a march on the rest of the field in the new Ferrari. He took 5 seconds off Clark and Moss in the first three laps. Despite his good start it was clear that Clark's engine was not at its best due to a piston problem, and he very soon returned to the pits for attention. Moss took five laps before getting his head down and starting to work on Ginther. Bonnier in the new Porsche keeping him

company. Gurney, Brooks, McLaren, Phil Hill, Graham Hill, von Trips and Surtees followed on some way behind, having their own seven car battle. Brabham, who started at the back of the grid, patiently waited for them to sort themselves out.

By the twelfth lap Moss was tight behind Ginther but Bonnier was finding the pace a little bit quick (fastest lap Ginther 1 min. 40) Graham Hill retired with fuel pump trouble, and, though he pushed his car to the pits, nothing could be done.

On lap 14 both Moss and Bonnier passed the Ferrari, Phil Hill had moved ahead of Gurney, then von Trips, Surtees, McLaren, Brooks and Brabham followed on. Moss began to pull away on his own, and when von Trips passed Gurney, the three Ferraris were together.

Quarter distance found Brabham in trouble with his engine blowing smoke. Clark was also running again at the rear of the field. Phil Hill passed Ginther and all three Ferraris began to pressure Bonnier. Moss at this

Above
Moss lifts a wheel at the top of the hill.

Below
Ginther in the Ferrari V6 leads Moss. The Ferrari went on to finish second.

37

An exhausted Stirling Moss at the end of his epic drive.

NINETEENTH
GRAND PRIX
OF MONACO
RESULTS

stage had a lead of 10 seconds and was consistently lapping below 1 min. 40 - remember he was giving away 25 b.h.p. to the Ferraris!

At 32 laps, the order was Moss (Lotus), Phil Hill (Ferrari), Bonnier (Porsche), Ginther (Ferrari), von Trips (Ferrari), McLaren (Cooper), Surtees (Cooper). Soon after this Surtees nipped by McLaren on the Gasworks Hairpin to take sixth place. Ginther put in his main effort, passed Bonnier and then pressed Phil Hill, which resulted in a reduction in Stirling's lead. By halfway it was down to 6 seconds and both Bonnier and von Tripps were burnt off.

Moss, in this situation, was at his best, making up for lack of power with sheer skill and enjoying every minute of it. The lead was reduced to 4 seconds by lap 60 - 40 laps to go! Bonnier's car could take no more punishment and retired with fuel pump problems. Moss maintained his lead by virtue of his ability to overtake the tail enders so much more quickly than either Hill or Ginther. Hill in fact appeared to be holding up Ginther's progress and when Ginther finally got by on lap 75, he immediately closed the gap on Moss to only 4 seconds. Incidentally, Ginther's lap record at this stage was 1 min. 36.3 - only just outside the old formula record.

In spite of all Ginther's efforts, Moss drove a faultless race and finally won his third Monaco Grand Prix by just over 3 seconds, with Phil Hill third.

1st	S.Moss	Lotus-Climax	lap 100	2 hr. 45 min. 50.1
2nd	P.R.Ginther	Ferrari 120 V6	lap 100	2 hr. 45 min. 53.7
3rd	P.Hill	Ferrari 60 V6	lap 100	2 hr. 46 min. 31.4
4th	W.von Trips	Ferrari 60 V6	lap 98	
5th	D.Gurney	Porsche 4 cyl.	lap 98	
6th	B.McLaren	Cooper-Climax	lap 95	
7th	M.Trintignant	Cooper-Climax	lap 95	
8th	C.Allison	Lotus-Climax	lap 93	
9th	H.Herrmann	Porsche 4 cyl.	lap 91	
10th	J.Clark	Lotus-Climax	lap 89	
11th	J.Surtees	Cooper-Climax	lap 68	
12th	J.Bonnier	Porsche 4 cyl.	lap 59	
13th	C.A.S.Brooks	B.R.M.-Climax	lap 54	

Fastest lap: P.R.Ginther (Ferrari) lap 84, and S. Moss (Lotus-Climax), lap 85, in 1 min. 36.3
117.570 k.p.h.

Retired: G.Hill *(B.R.M.-Climax)*, lap 12; J.Brabham *(Cooper-Climax)*, lap 39; M.May *(Lotus-Climax)*, lap 42

Development of engines for the new formula was still very limited at the beginning of 1962. Ferrari and B.R.M. were benefitting as a result of their investments but Porsche were still struggling to obtain sufficient power from their new 8-cylinder motor, and in fact seriously considered withdrawing from the Monaco race. Lotus were top of the queue for B.R.M. engines, but supply was very limited and they mainly had to rely on the Climax V8. The remainder were powered by Climax V8 if they were lucky, but often the old 4-cylinder.

ENTRIES

DRIVER	TEAM	CAR
J. Bonnier	Porsche	Porsche 4 cyl.
D Gurney	Porsche	Posche 8 cyl.
R. Ginther	Owen Racing	B.R.M. V8
G. Hill	Owen Racing	B.R.M. V8
B. McLaren	Cooper	Cooper-Climax V8
A. Maggs	Cooper	Cooper-Climax 4
J. Clark	Lotus	Lotus 25-Climax V8
T. Taylor	Lotus	Lotus 24-Climax V8
J. Brabham	Brabham	Lotus 24-Climax V8
J. Lewis	Ecurie Galloise	B.R.M. V8
R. Salvadori	Bowmaker	Lola-Climax V8
J. Surtees	Bowmaker	Lola-Climax V8
M. Trintignant	Walker	Lotus 24-Climax V8
M. Gregory	U.D.T.-Laystall	Lotus 24-B.R.M. V8
I. Ireland	U.D.T.-Laystall	Lotus 24-Climax V8
P. Hill	Ferrari	Ferrari-120 V6
L. Bandini	Ferrari	Ferrari-120 V6
W. Mairesse	Ferrari	Ferrari-120 V6
N. Vaccarella	S.S.S. Venezia	Lotus-Climax 4 cyl.
G. de Beaufort	Maarsbergen	Porsche-4 cyl.
J. Siffert	Suisse	Lotus-Climax 4 cyl.

Once again the Monaco grid was limited to 16 starters, with guaranteed entries for the works teams. This gave rise to some controversy since not all the

Bottom
Phil Hill in the Ferrari 120 degree V6

Below
Graham Hill's B.R.M. V8 failed while leading the race.

works teams could power both of their cars with the latest engine and as will be seen in the practice times, the second works car frequently kept out a much faster private entry. However, suggestions that the older works cars should qualify with the rest were ignored and eleven qualifiers found themselves fighting over six places on the grid.

Invited entries were Bonnier and Gurney for Porsche, Ginther and Graham Hill for B.R.M., McLaren and Maggs for Cooper, Clark and Taylor for Lotus, Phil Hill and Bandini or Mairesse for Ferrari. The qualifying battle was between - Brabham, driving for himself, Trintignant for Walker, Lewis for Ecurie Galloise, Salvadori and Surtees for Bowmaker (taking over from Yeoman Credit), Gregory and Ireland made up the U.D.T.-Laystall team, Vaccarella drove for S.S.S. Venezia, de Beaufort for Ecurie Maarsbergen, and Siffert for Ecurie Suisse.

1960 to 1962 was a time of change in G.P. motor racing. 1960 had seen a grid consisting of a mixture of front and rear-engined cars, and by 1961 and the introduction of the 1½-litre formula, the whole grid was rear-engined. At the same time Lotus introduced their new 'monocoque' cars, replacing the old space frame chassis with a

Above
Mirabeau Hairpin.

lightweight box like construction, which incorporated the fuel tanks, and onto which was bolted the engine, gearbox and suspension. The driver was in a new, almost prone position, which gave the car a much lower, sleeker profile. Later in 1962 saw the introduction of fuel injection on many engines, which, while not new, had not been widely used until then. This was the general pattern that was to be applied to most cars from the '60s onward.

Practice began on the Thursday with the two Hills, Clark, Surtees and Gurney setting the pace. The leading times were recorded by Clark, 1 min. 37.4, and Graham Hill, 1 min. 37.7. Friday practice was ruined by continuous rain and though most turned out to try their cars in the wet, their times were of no significance with only Graham Hill recording under two minutes.

Saturday afternoon saw the return of traditional Monaco weather and the final chance for the qualifiers. The lucky six were - Mairesse (Bandini took the Ferrari team's second invitation place), Brabham, Trintignant, Surtees and Salvadori. Of the non-qualifiers Lewis, Gregory and Siffert recorded times which would have gained them starting places under the old non-invitation system.

For a number of years after the war one of the resident characters at Monaco was the Race Director - Louis Chiron. Before the war he had been a driver of some considerable ability, with a Monaco win in 1931 with a Bugatti. Even as late as 1950 he had achieved a third place (in a Maserati) behind Fangio and Ascari. By the '60s he was using up his superfluous energies with the starting flag for the Grand Prix, and any other flag he

STARTING GRID

14	10	18
McLaren	**G.Hill**	**Clark**
1 min. 36.4	1 min. 35.8	1 min. 35.4

4	40
Gurney	**Mairesse**
1 min. 36.4	1 min. 36.4

34	30	22
Ireland	**Trintignant**	**Brabham**
1 min. 37.0	1 min. 36.8	1 min. 36.5

38	36
Bandini	**P. Hill**
1 min. 37.2	1 min. 37.1

8	26	28
Ginther	**Salvadori**	**Surtees**
1 min. 39.0	1 min. 38.5	1 min. 37.9

2	20
Bonnier	**T. Taylor**
1 min. 42.4	1 min. 40.0

16
Maggs
1 min. 42.7

41

Ginther, Trintignant and Ireland amongst the straw bales at Gasworks Hairpin.

could lay his hands on during the race! The resulting chaos was something every regular visitor to Monaco learned to live with; Chiron was a law unto himself!

Chiron's starting system was to raise the flag exactly 30 seconds before the off and, after a careful count down, drop the flag at zero, which sounds good and sensible. Unfortunately, in 1962 he lowered the flag some seconds too early, much to the surprise of the front row of the grid, who had scarcely engaged first gear! Mairesse however, who was creeping forward in the second row, shot forward, colliding with both Clark and Graham Hill before accelerating through to the Gasworks Hairpin. His Ferrari entered the bend much too fast and spun sideways on. The following cars of course found the road almost completely blocked. Clark stopped but Graham Hill and McLaren found their way through and led up the hill. At the same time Ginther's throttle stuck open going into the hairpin and he collided with Trintignant and Ireland, all three finishing in a heap among the straw bales on the outside of the bend. Only Ireland was able to motor back to the pits for repairs which put him back into the race.

42

Leader at the end of lap 1 was McLaren, followed by Graham Hill, Phil Hill, Bonnier, Bandini, Clark, Maggs, Brabham, Surtees, Salvadori, Mairesse and Taylor. By lap 7 the race had settled down and Graham Hill took the lead from McLaren and set about building a good lead. His main competition now came from Clark who had charged through into second place and, as always, was driving with great spirit. He closed up to within 1 second of the B.R.M., with a new lap record of 1 min. 35.5 on lap 42.

Hill was doing a 'Moss' in overtaking the tail enders, and in doing so was able to open up the lead to something more comfortable. By half way Clark was 15 seconds back and beginning to experience gear problems with his Lotus. Following on some way back were McLaren (Cooper), Brabham (Lotus), Phil Hill (Ferrari), Surtees (Lola), Bandini (Ferrari), Bonnier (Porsche), Mairesse (Ferrari) and Ireland (Lotus).

On lap 56 Clark's race was finished, his clutch having failed. Meanwhile Graham Hill's B.R.M. engine was beginning to sound sick and McLaren and Phil Hill were beginning to make inroads on his lead. Bandini and Surtees, while having their own private duel, unlapped themselves just before the B.R.M. failed completely on lap 93.

Phil Hill gave it all he had but McLaren coolly paced himself to the finish, crossing the line 1 second ahead. Bandini brought his Ferrari home in third place.

Bruce McLaren in the winning Cooper-Climax V8.

Bruce McLaren driving brilliantly to his first and only win. In later years he became a highly successful constructor of Grand Prix cars.

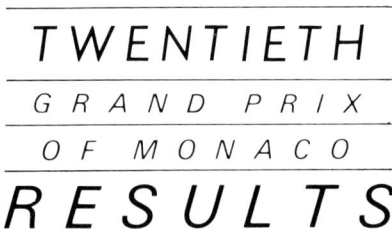

TWENTIETH
GRAND PRIX
OF MONACO
RESULTS

The new lap record of 1 min. 35.5. showed once again that the engineers aided by drivers of the calibre of Clark, had overcome the restrictions placed upon them by the administration. They in their turn could be consoled by the thought that the new formula had helped the development of the motor car another step forward.

1st	B.McLaren	Cooper-Climax V8	lap 100	2 hr. 46 min. 29.7
2nd	P.Hill	Ferrari 120-V6	lap 100	2 hr. 46 min. 31.0
3rd	L.Bandini	Ferrari 120-V6	lap 100	2 hr. 47 min. 53.8
4th	J.Surtees	Lola-Climax V8	lap 99	
5th	J.Bonnier	Porsche 4-cyl	lap 93	

Fastest lap: J.Clark (Lotus-Climax V8) lap 42, 1 min. 35.5 118.554 k.p.h. *(new record)*

Retired: R.Ginther *(B.R.M. V8)*, lap 1, crash; M.Trintignant *(Lotus-Climax V8)*, lap 1, crash; D.Gurney *(Porsche 8 cyl.)*, lap 1, crash; T.Taylor *(Lotus-Climax V8)*, lap 25, oil leak; A.Maggs *(Cooper-Climax 4)*, lap 44, mechanical; R.Salvadori *(Lola-Climax V8)*, lap 45, suspension; J.Clark *(Lotus-Climax V8)*, lap 56, clutch; I.Ireland *(Lotus-Climax V8)*, lap 64, fuel pump; J.Brabham *(Lotus-Climax V8)*, lap 78, crash; W.Mairesse *(Ferrari 120- V6)*, lap 91, engine; G.Hill *(B.R.M. V8)*, lap 93, engine.

The 21st Monaco Grand Prix was also the Grand Prix d'Europe, a title held by each national Grand Prix in its turn. One of the disadvantages of Monaco's early date in the season - more often than not it is the first race of the championship, - is that some of the current year's cars are either not ready in time or, because of the unforgiving nature of the circuit, not put at risk. The 1963 race was once again limited to 16 starters but probably because of the previous year's furore over slow, out-of-date works cars getting preference over faster privateers, only five drivers were guaranteed places. These were the past and present World Champions and previous winners of the race. Therefore Brabham, both Hills,

ENTRIES

DRIVER	TEAM	CAR
J. Brabham	Brabham	Brabham-Climax V8
D. Gurney	Brabham	Brabham-Climax V8
R. Ginther	B.R.M.	B.R.M. V8
G. Hill	B.R.M.	B.R.M. V8
B. McLaren	Cooper	Cooper-Climax V8
A. Maggs	Cooper	Cooper-Climax V8
J. Clark	Lotus	Lotus-Climax V8
T. Taylor	Lotus	Lotus-Climax V8
J. Bonnier	Walker	Cooper-Climax V8
J. Hall	B.R.P.	Lotus-B.R.M. V8
I. Ireland	B.R.P.	Lotus-B.R.M. V8
C. Amon	Parnell	Lola-Climax V8
M. Trintignant	Parnell	Lola-Climax V8
W. Mairesse	Ferrari	Ferrari V6
J. Surtees	Ferrari	Ferrari V6
B. Collomb	Collomb	Lotus-Climax V8
J. Siffert	Siffert	Lotus-B.R.M. V8

McLaren and Trintignant were on the grid regardless of car or time. As chance would have it they were each in a

45

STARTING GRID

9	6
Clark	**G. Hill**
1 min. 34.3	1 min. 35.0
21	5
Surtees	**Ginther**
1 min. 35.2	1 min. 35.2
14	4
Ireland	**Gurney**
1 min. 35.5	1 min. 35.8
20	7
Mairesse	**McLaren**
1 min. 35.9	1 min. 36.0
10	8
T. Taylor	**Maggs**
1 min. 37.2	1 min. 37.9
11	25
Bonnier	**Siffert**
1 min. 38.6	1 min. 39.4
12	17
Hall	**Trintignant**
1 min. 41.0	1 min 41.3
	3
	Brabham
	1 min. 44.7

different make of car. These were Brabham-Climax, B.R.M., A.T.S., Cooper-Climax and Lola-Climax respectively.

Of the works teams only Lotus suffered as a result of the new arrangement, having to qualify with the rest. Since only seventeen cars turned out for practice, only one was likely to be disappointed - all being well!

The first practice session, in perfect conditions, was led by Clark (Lotus-Climax) with 1 min. 35.3, with Graham Hill and Ginther's B.R.M.s settling in on 1 min. 37. Most of the others suffered teething troubles of one sort or another, the most serious being Brabham whose engine blew up in the biggest possible way and necessitated him flying back home to get it all put back together again.

Friday's practice was much more promising with most recording well under 1 min. 40, but again led by Clark with 1 min. 34.3. There was serious doubt about the ability of Collomb in this sort of company and it seemed unlikely that he would be allowed to start unless he could show considerable improvement on his best time of 1 min. 43.3. This he was unable to do, and the organisers took the sensible decision.

The final practice made little difference to the overall situation, Clark being happy to settle for his Friday time and his mechanics so untroubled by their cars that they were able to improve on their sun tans!

The grid layout was changed to an offset pairs formation as opposed to the old two/three/two formation. Brabham was relegated to the back row after giving his car to Gurney. Fortunately he was able to borrow a spare Lotus in order to take part - starting money taking precedence over competitiveness!

To everyone's relief Race Director Chiron got all fifteen cars away to a smooth start, unlike the previous year. Hill and Ginther led from Clark, Surtees and McLaren at a brisk pace. Even on a full load of fuel, virtually the whole field were lapping at under 1 min. 40. Clark made the first positive move on lap 5, passing Ginther and closing up on Graham Hill - another Lotus/B.R.M. duel was on the cards. For three laps Clark tried every way he knew to get by Hill, but Graham's perfect racing line frustrated him repeatedly. But persistence had to tell and Clark finally got by, only to make a mess of the Station Hairpin, running wide, and allowing both Hill and Ginther through. Still well in touch with the leaders were Surtees (Ferrari), McLaren (Cooper), Ireland (Lotus), Gurney (Brabham), Maggs

(Cooper) and Mairesse (Ferrari).

Clark once again passed Ginther and the duel recommenced. Hill always maintained the racing line and though Clark came through on the inside he was always out-accelerated from the bend.

Meanwhile Siffert, Bonnier and Hall were all in mechanical difficulties. Siffert's engine broke and he retired, soon followed by Hall with gearbox trouble. Brabham was being lapped by the whole pack of leaders, but he was responsible enough to keep well out of everyone's way.

On lap 17 Clark again took the lead and his superior cornering enabled him to draw away from Hill. The order was now Clark, Hill, Ginther, Surtees, McLaren, Ireland, Mairesse, Gurney and Maggs. Soon afterwards, Gurney was forced to retire and on lap 35 Trintignant pushed his Lola just too hard and blew the engine. The field was now reduced to eleven.

Nearing the half way point McLaren and Clark held the fastest laps with 1 min. 36.2, but this was surpassed by Clark on lap 48 with 1 min. 35.8. He now led by 9 seconds. Hill was now battling with Surtees, the former World Motorcycle Champion taking the lead for five laps before losing it again. After that effort his car was never quite the same and he began to drop back until Ginther and McLaren began to pressure him. Both passed him on lap 79. The order was now Clark, Hill, Ginther, McLaren, Surtees and only these were on the same lap, everyone else at least one lap behind.

With only a little over quarter distance to go Clark was out. A minor mechanical problem left him without gears, robbing him of that elusive Monaco victory. The remainder of the race was now a formality for the reliable B.R.M.s and both Hill and Ginther were so confident of their machinery that they kept up the same pace until the end. Hill had set a new record for the race, even though Surtees claimed the new lap record, unusually on the very last lap (his car having apparently found a new lease of life). The crowd had seen another great race with interest sustained to the end. Nobody leaves early at Monaco!

47

Prince Rainier, Princess Grace (the former Holywood film star Grace Kelly), and race winner Graham Hill stand for the national anthem.

TWENTY–FIRST
GRAND PRIX
OF MONACO
RESULTS

1st	G.Hill	B.R.M. V8	lap 100	2 hr. 41 min. 49.7
2nd	R.Ginther	B.R.M. V8	lap 100	2 hr. 41 min. 54.3
3rd	B.McLaren	Cooper-Climax V8	lap 100	2 hr. 42 min. 02.5
4th	J.Surtees	Ferrari V6	lap 100	2 hr. 42 min. 03.8
5th	A.Maggs	Cooper-Climax V8	lap 98	
6th	T.Taylor	Lotus-Climax V8	lap 98	
7th	J.Bonnier	Cooper-Climax V8	lap 94	
8th	J.Brabham	Lotus-Climax V8	lap 77	

Fastest lap: J.Surtees (Ferrari V6), lap 100, 1 min. 34.5 119.809 k.p.h. *(new record)*

Retired: J.Siffert *(Lotus-B.R.M. V8)*, lap 4, engine; J.Hall *(Lotus-B.R.M. V8)*, lap 21, gearbox; D.Gurney *(Brabham-Climax V8)*, lap 26, rear axle; M. Trintignant *(Lola-Climax V8)*, lap 35, engine; W.Mairesse *(Ferrari V6)*, lap 38, rear axle; I.Ireland *(Lotus-B.R.M. V8)*, lap 41, crashed; J.Clark *(Lotus-Climax V8)*, lap 78, gearbox.

As in 1963, few of the 1964 cars were prepared in time for Monaco - the first race of the new season. A good winter's work provided the latest B.R.M. V8s for Graham Hill and Ginther, and Brabham turned out his latest Climax V8 for himself and Gurney. The Cooper team showed up with two of their new cars but both were relatively untested. McLaren and Phil Hill were to drive, but in the race itself McLaren chose to drive his 1963 car. Ferrari provided three new cars for Surtees and Bandini as one might have expected, but pressure on the factory meant that they were underdeveloped. Arundell

ENTRIES

DRIVER	TEAM	CAR
P. Revson	Revson	Lotus-B.R.M. V8
B. Collomb	Collomb	Lotus-Climax V8
M. Trintignant	Trintignant	B.R.M. V8
J. Brabham	Brabham	Brabham-Climax V8
D. Gurney	Brabham	Brabham-Climax V8
R. Ginther	B.R.M.	B.R.M. V8
G. Hill	B.R.M.	B.R.M. V8
P. Hill	Cooper	Cooper-Climax V8
B. McLaren	Cooper	Cooper-Climax V8
P. Arundell	Lotus	Lotus-Climax V8
J. Clark	Lotus	Lotus-Climax V8
I. Ireland	B.R.P.	Lotus-B.R.M. V8
T. Taylor	B.R.P.	B.R.P.-B.R.M. V8
R. Anderson	Anderson	Brabham-Climax V8
C. Amon	Amon	Lotus-B.R.M. V8
M. Hailwood	Hailwood	Lotus-B.R.M. V8
J. Bonnier	Walker	Cooper-Climax V8
L. Bandini	Ferrari	Ferrari V6
J. Surtees	Ferrari	Ferrari V8
J. Siffert	Siffert	Lotus-B.R.M. V8

and Jim Clark were still in last year's Type 25 for Team Lotus, the new Type 33 having had a set back. The B.R.P. team were also in last year's 'mongrels': Ireland

49

STARTING GRID

12	5
J. Clark	**J. Brabham**
1 min. 34.0	1 min. 34.1
8	21
G. Hill	**J. Surtees**
1 min. 34.5	1 min. 34.5
6	11
D. Gurney	**P. Arundell**
1 min. 34.7	1 min. 35.5
20	7
L. Bandini	**R. Ginther**
1 min. 35.5	1 min. 35.9
9	10
P. Hill	**B. McLaren**
1 min. 35.9	1 min. 36.6
19	16
J. Bonnier	**R. Anderson**
1 min. 37.4	1 min. 38.0
4	15
M. Trintignant	**T. Taylor**
1 min. 38.1	1 min. 38.1
18	24
M. Hailwood	**J. Siffert**
1 min. 38.5	1 min. 38.7

in the Lotus-B.R.M. and Taylor the B.R.P.

The private entries were Amon and Hailwood in Lotus-B.R.M.s, Anderson in a brand new B.R.M. V8, Bonnier with the Walker Cooper-Climax V8, Trintignant a B.R.M. V8 1962, Revson a Lotus-B.R.M., Collomb a Lotus Climax V8, and Siffert a Lotus B.R.M. V8.

Practice over three days was dominated by the better prepared 1964 cars with the exception of Jim Clark, who, having missed the first day, clocked 1 min. 34 and took the pole position.

From the fall of the flag Clark was off, leaving everyone else to chase after his Lotus. His 'flat-out' opening lap immediately gained a clear 3 second lead over Brabham, Graham Hill, Gurney, Surtees and Ginther - the rest of the field out of sight! Clark maintained his superiority for the first 10 laps and the only other change amongst the leaders was by Gurney, who passed Hill and Brabham.

An early retirement was Taylor (B.R.P.) while Siffert (Lotus-B.R.M.) and Surtees (Ferrari) were also in mechanical trouble. McLaren's Cooper was also showing smoke signals of trouble to come, and, in fact retired on lap 18.

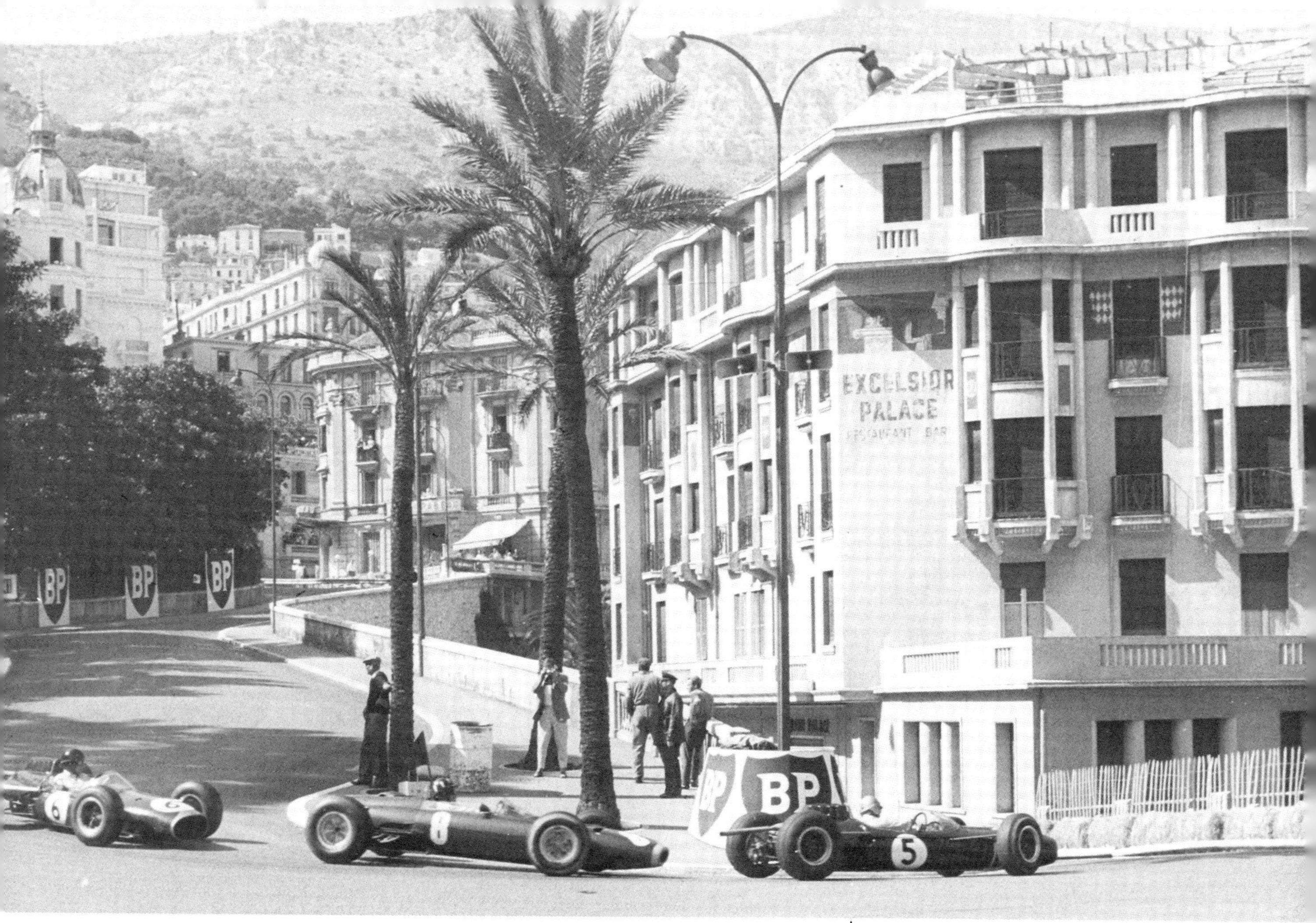

The leaders continued as if programmed until near quarter way, when it became evident that suspension problems were affecting the handling of the Lotus. Even so, he was not losing any time and the rest were making little impression on him. Brabham retired on lap 30, turning into the pits to save his new car from major damage. Therefore the order at this stage was Clark (Lotus), Gurney (Brabham), Hill (B.R.M.), Ginther (B.R.M.), Hill (Cooper), Bandini (Ferrari), Arundell (Lotus), Tintignant (B.R.M.), Bonnier (Cooper), Anderson (Brabham), Hailwood (Lotus) and Siffert (Lotus).

A loose anti-roll bar was evidently the cause of Clark's handling problems and, as the race approached the half way point, the bar was trailing and eventually broke off - Clark was called into the pits for a safety check and this allowed Gurney to take the lead. Graham Hill in a very much on-song B.R.M. was in second place and Clark had restarted a few seconds behind. Hill was able to fend off the challenge of Clark and in the process closed on Gurney. By the half way mark only two seconds covered the three leaders and it was clear that either Hill or Clark would soon be in the lead. Lap 53 and a new lap record of 1 min. 33.9 enabled Hill to pass Gurney - Clark was unable to follow until Gurney retired on lap 62, with a broken gearbox.

Above
Station Hairpin showing the road down from the Mirabeau Hotel. Brabham leads Hill, Guerney, Surtees and Ginther.

Left
Ginther driving the B.R.M. V8 to second place.

Below
Peter Arundell at the old chicane in a Lotus 25C Climax V8.

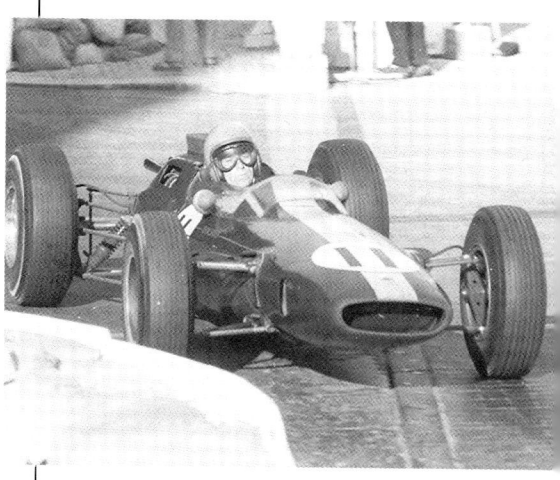

A determined looking Graham Hill sporting London Rowing Club colours on his helmet.

The only danger left to the dominant B.R.M. was the Lotus and, as the second half progressed, it was increasingly obvious that Clark's engine was failing and though he soldiered on until lap 90, his retirement was inevitable.

The untroubled B.R.M.s of Graham Hill and Ginther duly collected first and second places for the second year in a row, a just reward for the team's winter of preparation.

TWENTY–SECOND

GRAND PRIX

OF MONACO

RESULTS

1st	G.Hill	B.R.M. V8	lap 100	2 hr. 41 min. 19.5
2nd	R.Ginther	B.R.M. V8	lap 99	
3rd	P.Arundell	Lotus 25C-Climax	lap 97	
4th	J.Bonnier	Cooper-Climax V8	lap 96	
5th	M.Hailwood	Lotus 25-B.R.M. V8	lap 96	
6th	J.Siffert	Lotus 24-B.R.M. V8	lap 78	

Fastest lap: G.Hill (B.R.M. V8), lap 53, 1 min. 33.9 120.575 k.p.h.

Retired: T.Taylor *(B.R.P.-B.R.M. V8)*, petrol leak; J.Surtees *(Ferrari V8)*, gearbox; B.McLaren *(Cooper-Climax V8)*, oil leak; J.Brabham *(Brabham-Climax V8)*, injection. M.Trintignant *(B.R.M. V8)*, overheating; D.Gurney *(Brabham-Climax V8)*, gearbox; L.Bandini *(Ferrari V6)*, gearbox; P.Hill *((Cooper-Climax V8)*, rear suspension; R.Anderson *(Brabham-Climax V8)*, gearbox; J.Clark *(Lotus-Climax V8)*, engine.

'66 THE NEW 3 LITRE FORMULA

New formulas have proved in the past to be notoriously slow starters, even so the fans looked forward to the Monaco Grand Prix of 1966 and the début of the new cars. It was public knowledge that B.R.M. were developing a completely new H-16-cylinder engine but would it be ready in time? The other major teams were to turn out interim cars - developed 1965 chassis with engines adapted from other formulae.

Cooper were using a Maserati V-12 cylinder sports car engine fitted into a chassis built for the 16-cylinder Coventry-Climax engine, which had been abandoned.

ENTRIES

DRIVER	TEAM	CAR
B. McLaren	McLaren	McLaren-Ford V8
J. Clark	Lotus	Lotus-Climax V8
M. Spence	Parnell	Lotus-B.R.M. V8
J. Brabham	Brabham	Brabham-Repco V8
D. Hulme	Brabham	Brabham-Climax 4
R. Ginther	Cooper	Cooper-Maserati V12
J. Rindt	Cooper	Cooper-Maserati V12
G. Hill	Owen	B.R.M. V8
J. Stewart	Owen	B.R.M. V8
J. Siffert	Walker	Brabham-B.R.M. V8
R. Anderson	D.W. Racing	Brabham-Climax
L. Bandini	Ferrari	Ferrari V12
J. Surtees	Ferrari	Ferrari V12
J. Bonnier	Anglo-Suisse	Cooper-Maserati V12
G. Ligier	Ligier	Cooper-Maserati V12
R. Bondurant	Chamaco-Collect	B.R.M. V8

Coventry-Climax had in fact withdrawn from motor racing at the end of the previous season, much to everyone's regret.

Brabham was clearly concentrating on early success with a Repco-Brabham V8 sports car engine that would probably prove competitive for a couple of seasons, but had little development potential.

STARTING GRID

4	**17**
J. Clark	**J. Surtees**
1 min. 29.9	1 min. 30.1
12	**11**
J. Stewart	**G. Hill**
1 min. 30.3	1 min. 30.4
16	**8**
L. Bandini	**D. Hulme**
1 min. 30.5	1 min. 31.1
10	**15**
J. Rindt	**R. Anderson**
1 min. 32.2	1 min. 32.5
9	**2**
R. Ginther	**B. McLaren**
1 min. 32.6	1 min. 32.8
7	**6**
J. Brabham	**M. Spence**
1 min. 32.8	1 min. 33.5
14	**18**
J. Siffert	**J. Bonnier**
1 min. 34.4	1 min. 35.0
21	**19**
G. Ligier	**R. Bondurant**
1 min. 35.2	1 min. 37.3

Far Right
Jackie Stewart in the 2-litre B.R.M. interim special won the first of the new formula races.

Right
John Surtees in the new Ferrari V12 leads Stewart.

Bottom Right
Rindt in the ugly Cooper-Maserati V12 outbrakes Hill at Tabac.

The McLaren team had for some time been experimenting with Ford Indianapolis V8 engines with capacities reduced from 4.1-litres. A completely new monocoque chassis had been built to accept the engine, and the car promised to be strong and understressed with good early potential.

Ferrari delved into their Le Mans sports car workshop, taking their 3.3-litre V12 cylinder prototype engine for coupling with the 1965 monocoque/space frame Formula One chassis. Few doubted that it would be competitive.

The Monaco entry consisted of McLaren in his new car; Brabham in the new Repco-Brabham and Hulme in a 2.5-litre Climax-Brabham; Bandini and Surtees with new Ferraris and a spare 2.4-litre back up car; Ginther and Rindt in the new Cooper-Maserati V12s; and Ligier was also entered in a Cooper-Maserati.

B.R.M. turned out one H-16 car for Hill to try, but clearly he was more likely to race in the interim V8 2-litre, with Stewart as his team mate. Lotus were awaiting delivery of the B.R.M. H-16 engine for their new car, therefore Clark had a Type 33 Climax V8 2-litre car.

As practice started on the Thursday, these were the main contenders. After a number of years of 1½-litre engines, the new noise was most impressive, even from the bored out 1965 cars! Clark, Hill, Stewart, Hulme and Bandini found the tight circuit suited the older lighter cars, while of the new 3-litre competitors, the new Ferrari was quick in Surtees' hands. Jim Clark led the qualifiers with a remarkable 1 min. 29.9 lap - the first lap ever recorded below 1 min. 30 at Monaco!

The race was held on Sunday, May 22nd and started at 3 p.m. in ideal conditions. Clark's Lotus had gear problems and he was left stranded on the grid, and from pole position was the last away. Surtees in the 3-litre Ferrari led, closely followed by Stewart in the B.R.M., and the two soon opened up quite a gap on Hill, Hulme, Rindt and the rest. Stewart was giving Surtees no peace but was frustrated in his efforts to pass, and the duel continued for 13 laps before the Ferrari was forced to retire with a broken differential and Stewart led.

Rindt (Cooper), Hill (B.R.M.), Bandini (Ferrari), Clark (Lotus), Ginther (Cooper) and Spence (Lotus) were all still very much in the hunt, particularly Clark, who had very quickly moved through the field from last to fifth.

Besides Surtees, there were a number of early

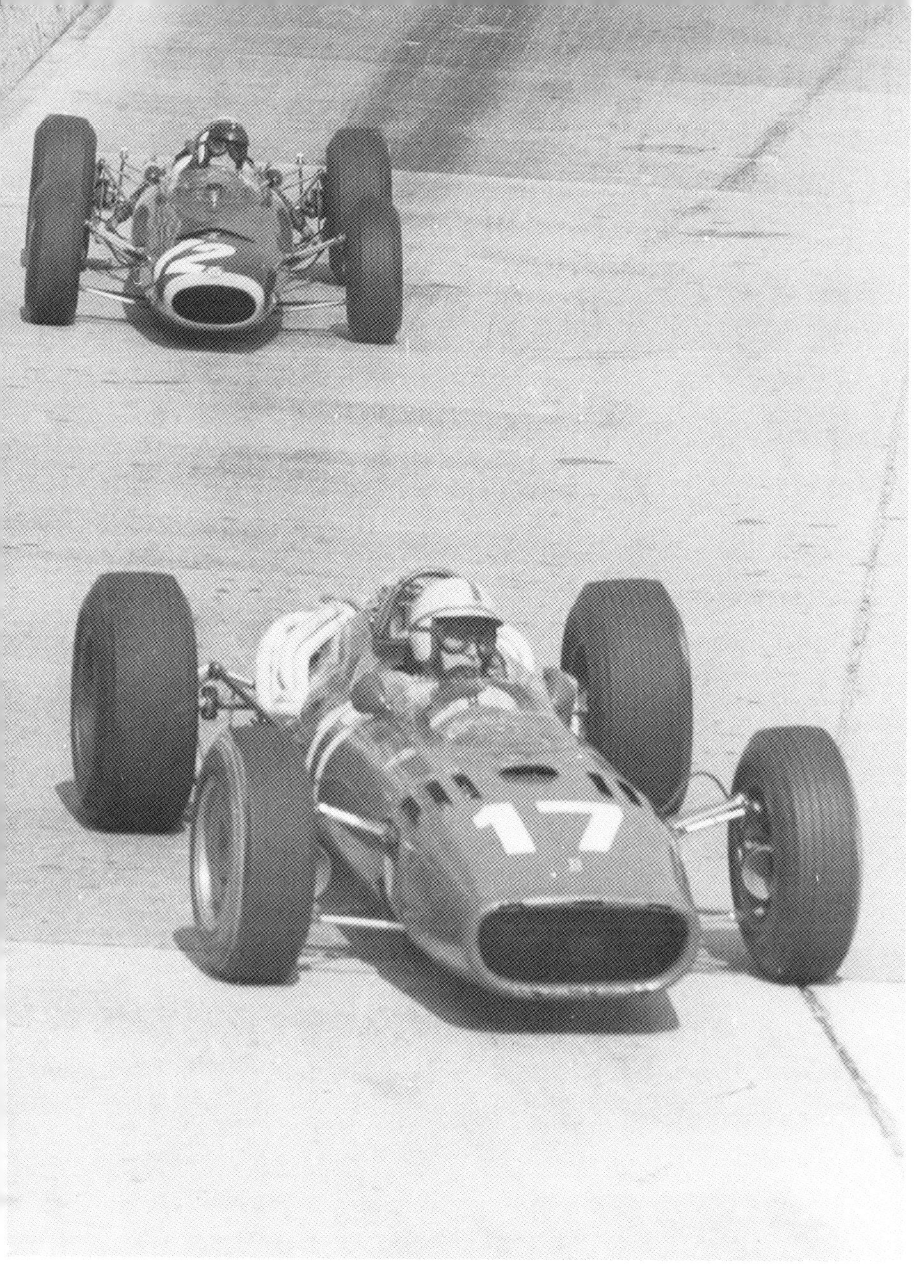

12
17

DUBONNET
arlboro
HERTZ
12

11
10

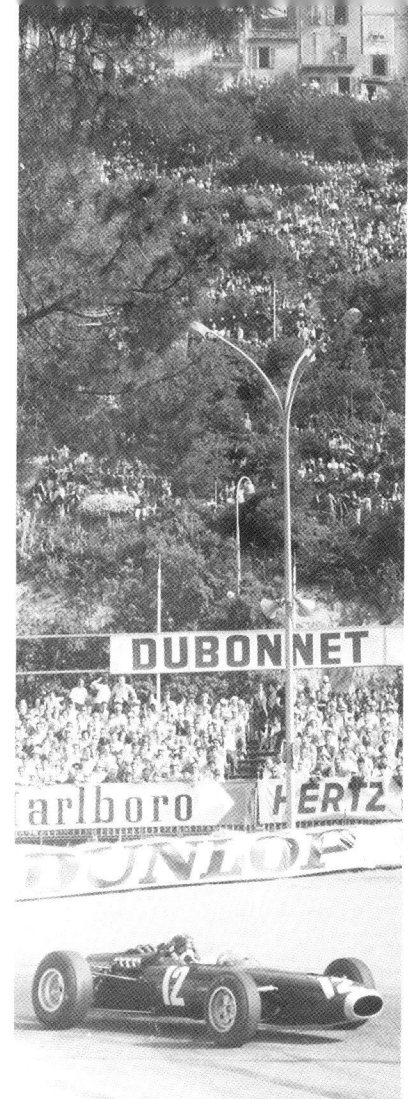

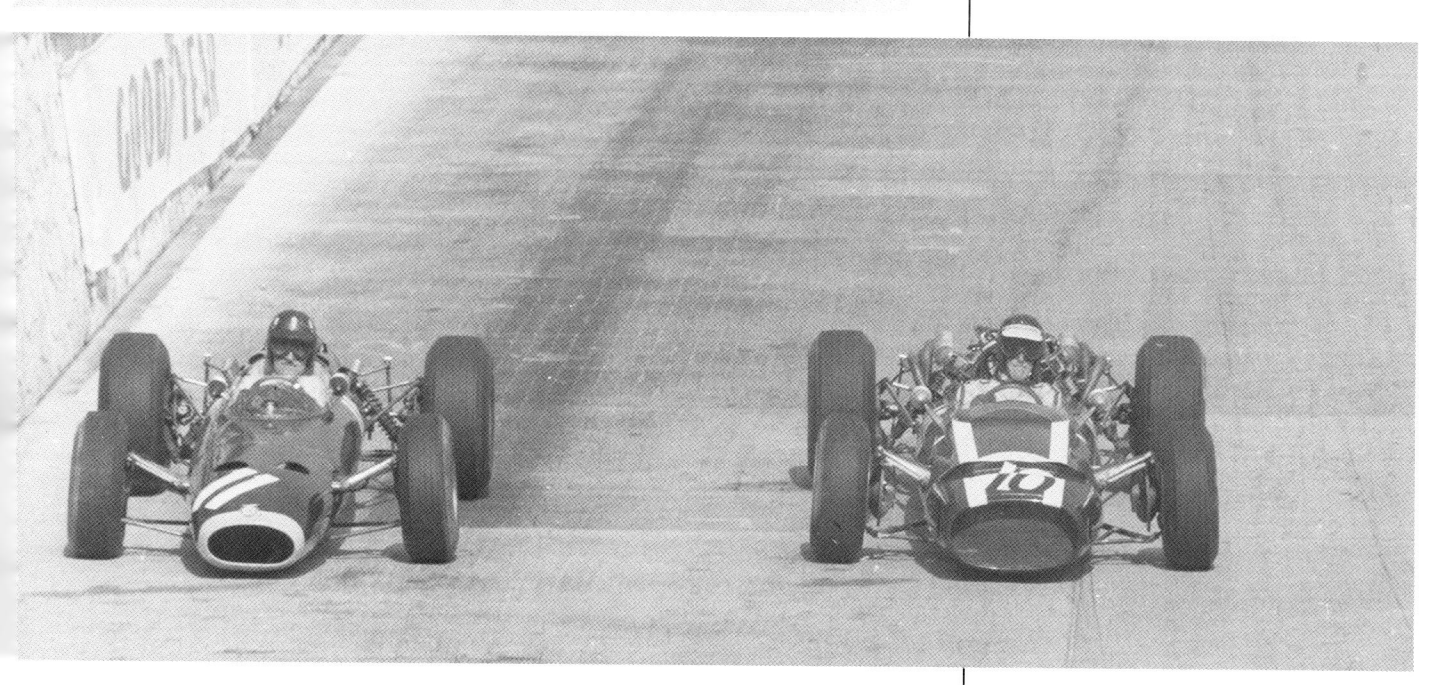

The winner - Stewart!

retirements. Hulme and Brabham were both out with drive train problems; Anderson was out; Siffert was in the pits and McLaren evidently in trouble also.

At about one third distance Bandini overtook Hill for third place and started to work on Rindt for second. Rindt, Bandini and Hill were nose to tail, with Clark slowly closing on them. Bandini and Hill eventually took Rindt, so that Clark's first problem was the big Cooper-Maserati. He was saved a great deal of hard work when, as the race approached half way, Rindt's engine lost power.

The order at half way was therefore - Stewart (B.R.M.), Bandini (Ferrari), Hill (B.R.M.), Clark (Lotus), Rindt (Cooper), Ginther (Cooper), Bondurant (B.R.M.), Bonnier (Cooper), Ligier (Cooper).

Stewart's lead was less than half a minute and, though he appeared comfortable, the main danger seemed likely to come from Clark, if he could ease past Hill and Bandini. On lap 61 the Lotus driver elbowed his way past Hill, but had no sooner got past, when the Lotus failed and he had no choice but to retire. The main danger gone, Stewart was able to control the rest of the race from the front, maintaining a 20 seconds lead over Bandini. Hill frightened himself by spinning his car on a hairpin bend, and from there on seemed to settle for third place.

Stewart duly took the chequered flag on B.R.M.'s behalf with a new record time for 100 laps of Monaco.

TWENTY-FOURTH
G R A N D   P R I X
O F   M O N A C O
R E S U L T S

1st	J.Stewart	B.R.M. V8 2 litre	lap 100	2 hr. 33 min. 10.5
2nd	L.Bandini	Ferrari V6 2.4 litre	lap 100	2 hr. 33 min. 50.7
3rd	G.Hill	B.R.M. V8 2 litre	lap 99	
4th	R.Bondurant	B.R.M. V8 2 litre	lap 95	

Fastest lap: L.Bandini (Ferrari V6), lap 90, 1 min. 29.8 126.080 k.p.h. *(new record)*

Retired: R.Anderson *(Brabham-Climax 4 cyl.),* lap 4; B.McLaren *(McLaren V8),* lap 10, oil leak: D.Hulme *(Brabham-Climax 4 cyl.),* lap 16, drive shaft coupling; J.Surtees *(Ferrari V12),* lap 17, rear axle; J.Brabham *(Brabham-Repco V8),* lap 18, gearbox; M.Spence *(Lotus-B.R.M. V8),* lap 35, rear suspension, J.Siffert *(Brabham-B.R.M. V8),* lap 36, clutch; J.Rindt *(Cooper-Maserati V12),* lap 56, engine, J.Clark *(Lotus-Climax V8),* lap 61, rear suspension; R.Ginther *(Cooper-Maserati V12),* lap 81, drive shaft

In the early days of the 3-litre formula there was some danger that Monaco might become a race for 'specials'. Undoubtedly the smaller, more nimble 2/2½-litre cars could more than hold their own around the streets, and until the new 3-litre cars were more developed and had established some reliability, there was a strong case for entering a 'special'. In 1966 all the teams were keen to try out their machinery but the '67 entry included a 2-litre B.R.M. for Stewart, with the new H 16 car for their second driver, Spence. Lotus had entered 2-litre Type 33s for Clark and Graham Hill (the

ENTRIES

DRIVER	TEAM	CAR
J. P. Beltoise	Matra	Matra-Cosworth FVA
J. Servoz-Gavin	Matra	Matra-Cosworth FVA
J. Stewart	B.R.M.	B.R.M. V8
M. Spence	B.R.M.	B.R.M. H16
P. Courage	Parnell	B.R.M. V8
J. Surtees	Honda	Honda V12
J. Brabham	Brabham	Brabham-Repco V8
D. Hulme	Brabham	Brabham-Repco V8
J. Rindt	Cooper	Cooper-Maserati V12
P. Rodriguez	Cooper	Cooper-Maserati V12
J. Clark	Lotus	Lotus-Climax V8
G. Hill	Lotus	Lotus 33-B.R.M. V8
R. Anderson	Anderson	Brabham-Climax 4
B. McLaren	McLaren	McLaren-B.R.M. V8
J. Siffert	Walker	Cooper-Maserati V12
L. Bandini	Ferrari	Ferrari V12
C. Amon	Ferrari	Ferrari V12
R. Ginther	A.A.R.	Eagle-Weslake V12
D. Gurney	A.A.R.	Eagle-Weslake V12

new Cosworth-Ford V8 was as yet unavailable). McLaren entered a 2-litre B.R.M. engined car for himself. Parnell entered Courage with a 2-litre B.R.M., while the two Matra entries for Beltoise and Servoz-Gavin were Formula Two cars.

61

STARTING GRID

8	18
J. Brabham	**L. Bandini**
1 min. 27.6	1 min. 28.3
7	9
J. Surtees	**D. Hulme**
1 min. 28.4	1 min. 28.8
12	4
J. Clark	**J. Stewart**
1 min. 28.8	1 min. 29.0
23	14
D. Gurney	**G. Hill**
1 min. 29.3	1 min. 29.9
17	16
J. Siffert	**B. McLaren**
1 min. 30.0	1 min. 30.0
2	5
J. Servoz-Gavin	**M. Spence**
1 min. 30.4	1 min. 30.6
6	20
P. Courage	**C. Amon**
1 min. 30.6	1 min. 30.7
10	11
J. Rindt	**P. Rodriguez**
1 min. 30.8	1 min. 32.4

Top Right
Bandini overtakes Surtees in the Honda V12.

Below
Bandini in the Ferrari V12 leads Brabham and the field up the hill from Ste. Devote. Bandini lost his life in a crash late in the race.

For the first time Monaco welcomed the Eagle-Weslake team with drivers Ginther and Gurney. Honda were back with their V12 cylinder cars for Surtees. Crafty Jack Brabham had three of his Repco cars for himself and Hulme to choose from.

Undoubtedly the ugliest of the 3-litre cars had to be the Cooper-Maserati. Cooper had entries for Rindt and Rodriguez and though private entries had been made for Bonnier and Ligier, neither turned up. But Siffert arrived with Walker's Cooper-Maserati and Anderson with his own Brabham 2.7-litre Climax.

This year's race was not the official first of the season - the South African Grand Prix had been held back in January - but from a technical point of view, Monaco was the first race with 1967 machinery. This was the first opportunity to compare progress against the 1966 result. So, as practice commenced, all had in mind Clark's 1 min. 29.9 and particularly Surtees' 1 min. 30.1 qualifying laps.

On the first day only Stewart was below 1 min. 30 in his 'special', but the big cars were going well and after three days of practice 1 min. 31 meant a spectator seat in the stand!

Right
McLaren, Hill and Rindt.

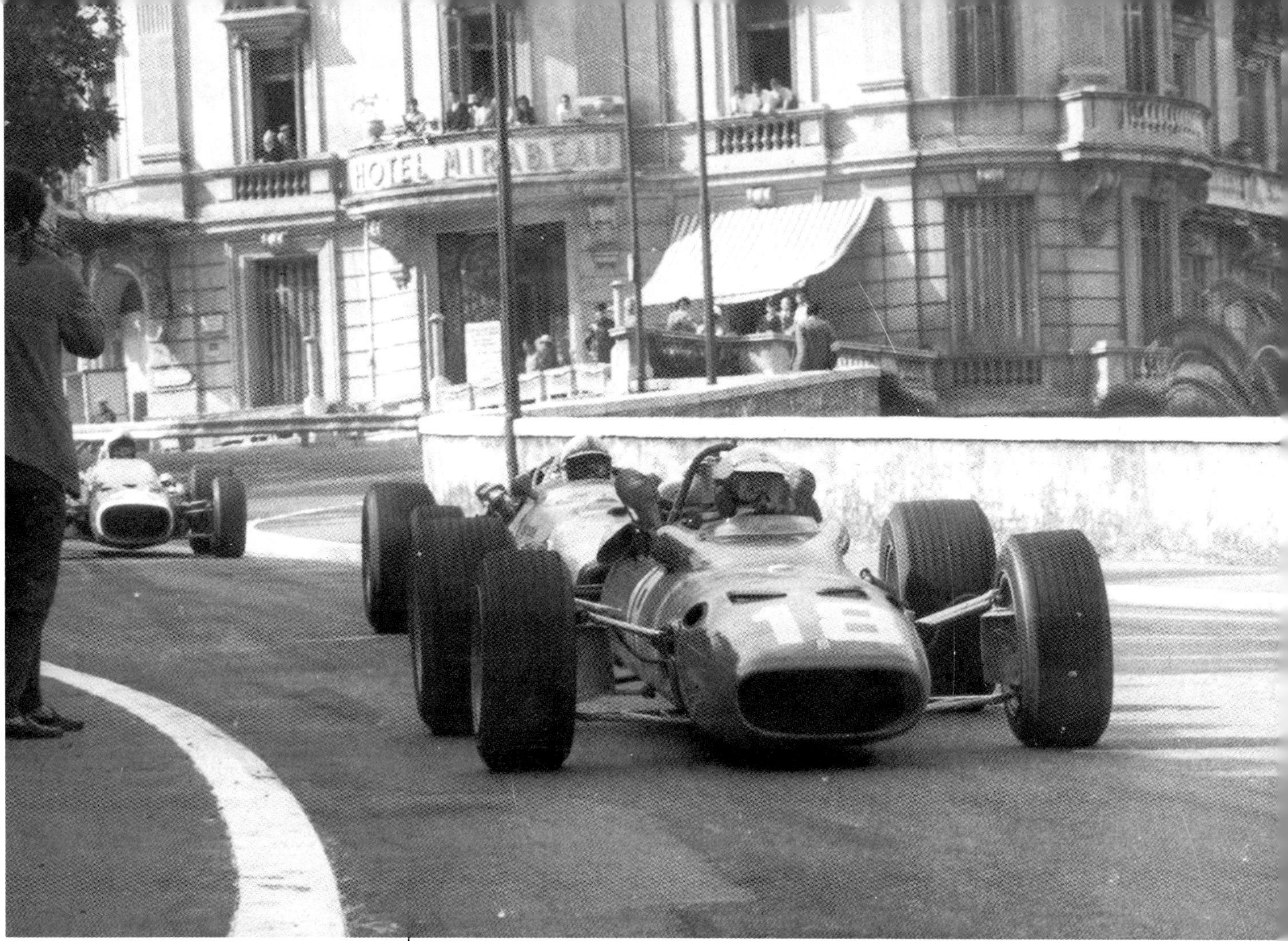
HOTEL MIRABEAU
18

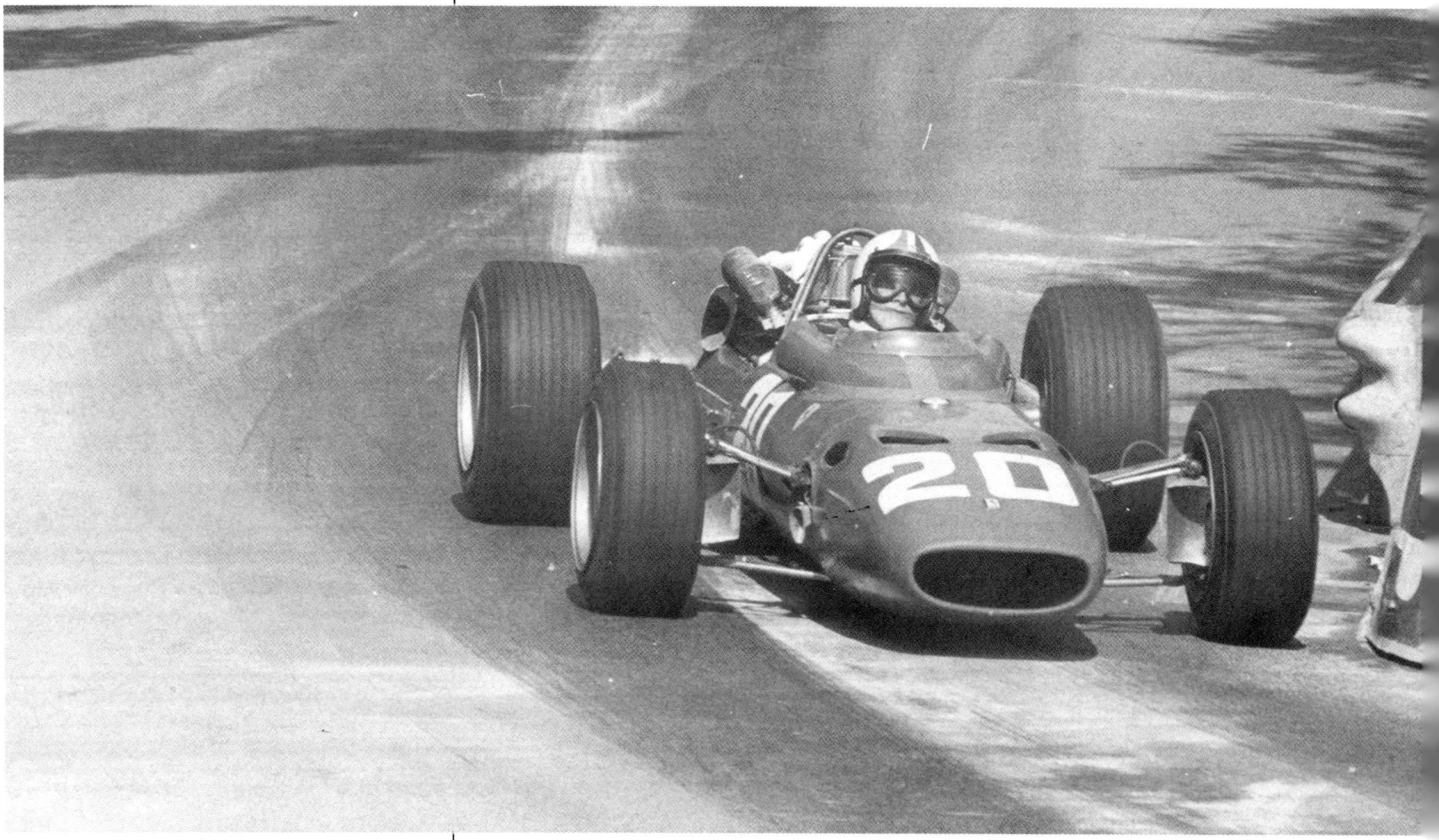
20

Particularly interesting was the performance of Surtees in the Honda and both Stewart and Spence in the H-16 B.R.M. Gurney also went very quickly in the pretty Eagle-Weslake, qualifying for the fourth row of the starting grid.

One small adjustment had been made to the course. The Start/Finish line was now moved along almost to Ste. Devote to allow a longer sprint for the line after the Gasworks Hairpin.

Chiron got everyone away to a good start and Bandini in the Ferrari out-dragged Brabham to the first corner which was fortunate since the Brabham blew a hole in its engine, spun and was lucky not to take out half the charging field on the first lap. However, only Siffert collided with him and he only slightly damaged his radiator. Bandini, Hulme, Stewart, Surtees and Gurney led the rest.

On the second lap Clark lost control of his Lotus on some of Brabham's oil but was able to rejoin the race at the rear. Hulme and Stewart caught and passed Bandini who had not taken full advantage of all the excitement behind him.

On lap five Gurney charged past both Surtees and Bandini before his engine let him down, and the lone Eagle was out. One lap later Stewart passed Hulme, so the order was now Stewart (B.R.M.), Hulme (Brabham), Bandini (Ferrari), Surtees (Honda), McLaren (McLaren), Rindt (Cooper), Hill (Lotus), Amon (Ferrari), Clark (Lotus), Spence (B.R.M.). Stewart's lead lasted until he retired with mechanical problems on lap 15. Rindt had also retired with gearbox trouble. By quarter distance Surtees' Honda was clearly in trouble and he was unable to maintain the pace. McLaren moved through to third place and, soon after, the charging Clark also passed the Honda and claimed fourth. Clark then set about catching McLaren but his Monaco jinx was to strike again when on lap 43 he spun into a wall and wrecked the rear end of the Lotus. The half way order was Hulme (Brabham), Bandini (Ferrari), McLaren (McLaren), Amon (Ferrari), Hill (Lotus), Spence (B.R.M.), Rodriguez (Cooper), Courage (B.R.M.), and Siffert (Cooper) restarted but many laps behind. For the next 20 laps the order remained unchanged until Courage spun and was forced to retire, and McLaren lost time in the pits with electrical problems.

Monaco is a great test of both driver and machine, and though notoriously unforgiving, there have not been too many major accidents over the years. On lap 82 Ban-

Above
Hulme, the eventual winner, passes the pits.

Top left
Bandini and Surtees charge through the Mirabeau.

Left
Chris Amon (Ferrari V12).

65

Hulme's fine win in the Brabham Repco V8 was overshadowed by Bandini's death.

dini lost control of his Ferrari after the chicane, hit some straw bales and the car turned over and burst into flames. The driver was badly burned and later died in hospital.

Hulme duly completed the 100 laps to win but the death of Bandini saddened everyone.

This was also to be Jim Clark's last Monaco Grand Prix. He was killed in the early part of 1968 while racing at Hockenheim in a relatively minor event. Clark never won at Monaco although he was almost always in contention.

TWENTY–FIFTH
GRAND PRIX
OF MONACO
RESULTS

1st	D.Hulme	Brabham-Repco	lap 100	2 hr. 34 min. 34.3
2nd	G.Hill	Lotus 33-B.R.M. V8	lap 99	
3rd	C.Amon	Ferrari V12	lap 98	
4th	B.McLaren	McLaren-B.R.M. V8	lap 97	
5th	P.Rodriguez	Cooper-Maserati	lap 96	
6th	M.Spence	B.R.M. H16	lap 96	

Fastest lap: J.Clark (Lotus 33-Climax V8), lap 38, 1 min. 29.5   126.502 k.p.h. *(new record)*

Retired: J.Brabham *(Brabham-Repco V8)*, lap 1, engine; J.Servoz-Gavin *(Matra-Cosworth 1600)*, lap 2, injection unit drive; D.Gurney *(Eagle-Weslake V12)*, lap 5, fuel pump drive; J.Stewart *(B.R.M. V8)*, lap 15, crown-wheel; J.Rindt *(Cooper-Maserati V12)*, lap 15, gearbox; J.Siffert *(Cooper-Maserati V12)*, lap 32, engine; J.Surtees *(Honda V12)*, lap 33, engine; J.Clark *(Lotus-Climax V8)*, lap 43, rear shock-absorber; P. Courage *(B.R.M. V8)*, lap 64, spun and stalled; L.Bandini *(Ferrari V12)*, lap 82, crashed.

This was a significant year in the history of the Monaco Grand Prix and of motor racing. The previous year the motor racing public had been introduced to the new Ford-Cosworth V8 engine in the Lotus. The new Lotus had won on its début race at Zandvoort when driven by Jim Clark, and the car had not even turned a wheel before the practice sessions! Now the Monaco public were to see this remarkable car and the engine that was to become probably the most successful racing engine ever built.

Also notable was the appearance of spoilers or wings on the Lotus. The introduction of aerodynamic aids was

ENTRIES

DRIVER	TEAM	CAR
J.P. Beltoise	Matra	Matra V12
J. Brabham	Brabham	Brabham-Repco V8
J. Rindt	Brabham	Brabham-Repco V8
P. Rodriguez	B.R.M.	B.R.M. V12
L. Scarfiotti	Cooper	Cooper-B.R.M. V12
L. Bianchi	Cooper	Cooper-B.R.M. V12
J. Surtees	Honda	Honda V12
G. Hill	Lotus	Lotus-Cosworth V8
J. Oliver	Lotus	Lotus-Cosworth V8
J. Servoz-Gavin	Tyrrell	Matra-Cosworth V8
D. Hulme	McLaren	McLaren-Cosworth V8
B. McLaren	McLaren	McLaren-Cosworth V8
R. Attwood	Parnell	B.R.M. V12
P. Courage	Parnell	B.R.M. V12
J. Siffert	Walker	Lotus-Cosworth V8
J. Bonnier	Bonnier	McLaren-B.R.M. V12
D. Gurney	A.A.R.	A.A.R.-Eagle V12
S. Moser	Vogele	Brabham-Repco V8

to make a considerable difference to the appearance of the Grand Prix car in the following years.

Changes to the circuit at Monaco were usually minor and infrequent. After Bandini's dreadful crash the

A close up of Graham Hill

STARTING GRID

9	11
G. Hill	**J. Servoz-Gavin**
1 min. 28.2	1 min. 28.8

17	8
J. Siffert	**J. Surtees**
1 min. 28.8	1 min. 29.1

3	15
J. Rindt	**R. Attwood**
1 min. 29.2	1 min. 29.6

14	1
B. McLaren	**J-P. Beltoise**
1 min. 29.6	1 min. 29.7

4	12
P. Rodriguez	**D. Hulme**
1 min. 30.4	1 min. 30.4

16	2
P. Courage	**J. Brabham**
1 min. 30.6	1 min. 31.2

10	7
J. Oliver	**L. Bianchi**
1 min. 31.7	1 min. 31.9

6	19
L. Scarfiotti	**D. Gurney**
1 min. 32.9	1 min. 32.9

chicane had been moved further away from the tunnel and made more severe in an effort to slow the traffic down at this point. Most of the drivers felt that the change would be of little consequence. More significant was the reduction of the race from the traditional 100 laps to 80, a move that was resented by most of the traditionalists.

The most important absentee was the Ferrari team, without explanation, but everyone assumed that it was a sign of respect for Bandini. The major contenders were Matra with one car for Beltoise; Brabham with Rindt as his new team mate; B.R.M. had Rodriguez and Attwood; Cooper had Scarfiotti and Bianchi; Honda again with Surtees; the Lotus team had Hill and now Oliver; McLaren two cars for Hulme and himself; and Gurney in the AAR-Eagle; Tyrrell-Matra had entered Servoz-Gavin; Parnell entered Courage; Walker entered Siffert; Vogele entered Moser; and finally Bonnier was in his own car.

The target practice time was Jack Brabham's 1967 time of 1 min. 27.6. With ten V12 powered cars in action early on, the noise was memorable! But V8s still seemed most effective with Hill, Servoz-Gavin and Siffert all below 1 min. 29, all of course Ford Cosworth powered. Of the V12s only Surtees got close with 1 min. 29.1. Bonnier and Moser failed to qualify.

Chiron got the sixteen starters away to a ragged start with Servoz-Gavin showing Hill the way. The Frenchman, encouraged by a partisan crowd, made the most of his moment of glory, using most of the road. Hill did not press, expecting him to come to grief at any moment. Siffert, Surtees and Rindt were therefore in close attendance. Two cars did not survive the first lap due to a coming together in the tunnel - McLaren and Oliver.

Much to the relief of everyone on the track, the Matra could not take the thrashing it was receiving from its driver and Servoz-Gavin retired after three laps. So the order was now Hill (Lotus), Siffert (Lotus), Surtees (Honda), Rindt (Brabham), Attwood (B.R.M.), Rodriguez (B.R.M.), Beltoise (Matra), Brabham (Brabham), Gurney (Eagle), Hulme (McLaren), Bianchi (Cooper) and finally Scarfiotti (Cooper).

And so the pattern was set. Hill controlled the race from the front, lapping smoothly and faultlessly, and one by one the remainder eliminated themselves! Only Attwood in the B.R.M. came away with any credit having stayed with the leader all the way, although unable to mount any real challenge.

Above
Servoz-Gavin driving in the lead, but his race was only to last for three laps.

Left
Hill, Siffert, Surtees, Rindt, Attwood, Rodriguez.

Bottom left
Enlarged air intakes to help cooling are sometimes necessary at Monaco. This is Bianchi (Cooper-B.R.M.).

69

Above
Attwood was the only driver on the same lap as the winner at the finish.

Right
A serene Princess Grace with Graham Hill once again.

Brabham went out on lap 8, Rindt crashed on lap 9, Gurney pulled out on lap 10 after a thoroughly miserable time. Siffert retired on lap 12, Beltoise also, Courage on lap 14 and Rodriguez on lap 17. Surtees also retired on lap 17. With less than a quarter of the race gone, eleven of the sixteen were out. Perhaps it was a good decision to have an 80 lap race after all!

Hulme in fact managed to rejoin the race after a lengthy stop and just managed to complete enough laps to get his championship points.

One has to admit that this was not one of the most memorable years at Monaco!

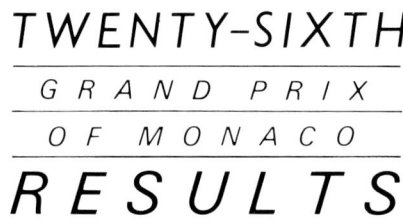

TWENTY-SIXTH
G R A N D   P R I X
O F   M O N A C O
R E S U L T S

1st	G.Hill	Lotus 49-Cosworth	lap 80	2 hr. 00 min. 32.3
2nd	R.Attwood	B.R.M. V12	lap 80	2 hr. 00min. 34.5
3rd	L.Bianchi	Cooper-B.R.M. V12	lap 76	
4th	L.Scarfiotti	Cooper-B.R.M. V12	lap 76	
5th	D.Hulme	McLaren-Cosworth	lap 73	

Fastest lap: R.Attwood (B.R.M. V12), lap 80, 1 min. 28.1, 128.513 k.p.h. *(new record)*

Retired: B.McLaren *(McLaren-Cosworth V8)* lap 1, accident; J.Oliver *(Lotus-Cosworth V8)*, lap 1, accident; J.Servoz-Gavin *(Matra MS10-Cosworth V8)* lap 4, drive shaft; J.Brabham *(Brabham-Repco V8)* lap 8, suspension; J.Rindt *(Brabham-Repco)* lap 9, accident; D.Gurney *(A.A.R.-Eagle V12)*, lap 10, engine; J.Siffert *(Lotus 49-Cosworth V8)*, lap 12, crown-wheel and pinion; J-P.Beltoise *(Matra V12)* lap 12, front suspension; P.Courage *(B.R.M. V12)* lap 14, broken chassis; P.Rodriguez *(B.R.M. V12)*, lap 17, accident; J.Surtees *(Honda V12)* lap 17, gearbox.

Three full seasons had been completed with the 3-litre formula. The interim specials had served their purpose and were now obsolete, and the major teams all had firm ideas of the way to go. The innovative H-16 B.R.M. engine had regretably been abandoned and more teams were turning over to the Ford-Cosworth V8 power plant. This was the beginning of the so-called 'kit car', when it was said that anyone could build a competitive Formula One car if they had four wheels, a monocoque chassis and the Cosworth engine. Though hardly meant seriously, there was a grain of truth in it. Because of the domination of one engine, teams had to find the minute variation to the norm that would give them an edge over the opposition.

ENTRIES

DRIVER	TEAM	CAR
G. Hill	Lotus	Lotus-Cosworth V8
R. Attwood	Lotus	Lotus-Cosworth V8
D. Hulme	McLaren	McLaren-Cosworth V8
B. McLaren	McLaren	McLaren-Cosworth V8
J. Brabham	Brabham	Brabham-Cosworth V8
J. Ickx	Brabham	Brabham-Cosworth V8
J. Stewart	Matra	Matra-Cosworth V8
J-P. Beltoise	Matra	Matra-Cosworth V8
J. Siffert	Walker	Lotus-Cosworth V8
P. Rodriguez	Parnell	B.R.M. V12
C. Amon	Amon	Ferrari V12
V. Elford	Antique Automobiles	Cooper-Maserati V12
J. Surtees	B.R.M.	B.R.M. V12
J. Oliver	B.R.M.	B.R.M. V12
P. Courage	Williams	Brabham-Cosworth V8
S. Moser	Moser	Brabham-Cosworth V8

Aerofoils had made an appearance on some cars the previous season, which some thought was not in the spirit of Grand Prix motor racing. The C.S.I., the governing body, seemed undecided over the matter, and their

STARTING GRID

7	11
J. Stewart	**C. Amon**
1 min. 24.6	1 min. 25.0
8	1
J-P. Beltoise	**G. Hill**
1 min. 25.4	1 min. 25.8
9	14
J. Siffert	**J. Surtees**
1 min. 26.0	1 min. 26.0
6	5
J. Ickx	**J. Brabham**
1 min. 26.3	1 min. 26.4
16	2
P. Courage	**R. Attwood**
1 min. 26.4	1 min. 26.5
4	3
B. McLaren	**D. Hulme**
1 min. 26.7	1 min. 26.8
15	10
J. Oliver	**P. Rodriguez**
1 min. 28.4	1 min. 30.5
17	12
S. Moser	**V. Elford**
1 min. 30.5	1 min. 32.8

Top Right
Stewart, seen here leading Amon, set the lap record but it was not made official because he did not finish!

Right
Courage at Tabac in the Brabham Cosworth V8. Note the prominent oil cooler and front wings.

rulings were unclear. Practice for the '69 Monaco was chaotic with wings banned initially which were not part of the bodywork. This meant that front wings were legal but rear wings were not! The resulting row ended with the first day's practice times being disregarded and the teams hastily trying to rebalance their cars in time for the second day of practice. Finally, wings attached to the chassis were allowed and everyone could get down to the serious business of winning a Grand Prix. The whole thing seemed totally unnecessary since on the low speed circuits the wings had little effect anyway.

The teams were Hill and Attwood in the Type 49 Lotus-Cosworth V8s for Lotus, Hulme and McLaren driving McLaren's own McLaren-Cosworth V8s, and Brabham and Ickx in Brabham-Cosworth V8s for, of course Team Brabham. Stewart and Beltoise were in the Matra-Cosworth V8s, Surtees and Oliver in the B.R.M. V12s, while Rodriguez was driving the Parnell B.R.M. V12. Siffert again drove the Lotus-Cosworth V8 for Walker/Durlacher. Frank Williams entered Courage in his Brabham-Cosworth V8. Moser had a private entry with a Brabham-Cosworth V8 special and Vic Elford made his first appearance in a Cooper-Maserati V12, appropriately entered by Antique Automobiles Ltd! Ferrari still seemed to be disenchanted with Monaco and had no official entry but Amon had a private entry with the current V12 team car, and was clearly well supported by Maranello.

The lap record currently stood at 1 min. 28.1 from the previous year's race (Attwood), and in spite of the chaos over the wings, everyone got in the mood and there was furious competition for the best starting grid positions. Stewart took pole position with 1 min. 24.6 and a highly competitive race seemed in prospect.

On a warm, cloudy Sunday the race was started by the new Race Director, Paul Frere. Stewart and Amon were off! They rocketed away from the rest of the field with the same crazy enthusiasm as in practice. Hill dropped into third and was not tempted to chase them. Ickx, Courage and Siffert followed on.

The two leaders were setting an unnecessarily fast pace, particularly Stewart who was even leaving Amon behind, and he was well clear of Hill and the rest. As Graham Hill later admitted, he had decided to play a waiting game and he gambled that neither Stewart or Amon could last the race at that sort of pace.

On lap 10 Brabham had an incredible escape when in collision with Surtees before the tunnel. With one

72

Above
**Rear view of the famous Cosworth V8
in Siffert's Lotus.**

Overleaf

Left
Surtees, Ickx, Courage, Brabham.

Top right
**A fine shot of Graham Hill and the
Lotus-Cosworth V8 - driving to his fifth
win at Monaco.**

Right
**The steepness of the hill down from the
tunnel can be clearly seen in this
picture. The cars are braking from
about 170 m.p.h. at this point.
Surtees ahead of Brabham, McLaren
and Attwood.**

Shell
GOLD LEAF
TEAM LOTUS
Ford
STP
Firestone
LOTUS
FORD

ONE
FERODO
MARTINI
Marlboro
BP
BP
Marlboro
AUTOBIANCHI

wheel missing and no brakes he three-wheeled through the tunnel, finally managing to stop on the other side. Neither driver was hurt!

By lap 19 Amon was out with a broken differential and Stewart, eased back to save the car, under orders from the pits. He really was very safe at this stage. Hill was a long way back in second and not showing any signs of wanting to risk his hastily built Lotus.

Beltoise (Matra) was third and the remainder were in the order Ickx (Brabham), Courage (Brabham), Siffert (Lotus), McLaren (McLaren), Attwood (Lotus), Hulme (McLaren), Elford (Cooper).

"All he had to do was stay on the road" — so they say! The Matra - in the lead and being driven relatively gently - broke a drive shaft and Stewart was out on lap 21. Beltoise had also retired with the same problem, so Hill, Ickx and Courage now found themselves 1, 2 and 3.

Graham Hill had too much experience of Monaco to throw this golden opportunity away, and though Ickx and Courage gave the crowd lots of entertainment, they were only racing each other. Hill was once again controlling the race from the front. This was the master of Monaco demonstrating how this race should be driven, by doing just enough, and his reward was an unprecedented fifth victory. Truly a race for the connoisseur.

TWENTY-SEVENTH
GRAND PRIX
OF MONACO
RESULTS

1st	G.Hill	Lotus-Cosworth	lap 80	1 hr. 56 min. 59.4
2nd	P.Courage	Brabham-Cosworth	lap 80	1 hr. 57 min. 16.7
3rd	J.Siffert	Lotus-Cosworth V8	lap 80	1 hr. 57 min. 34.0
4th	R.Attwood	Lotus-Cosworth V8	lap 80	1 hr. 57 min. 52.3
5th	B.McLaren	McLaren-Cosworth	lap 79	
6th	D.Hulme	McLaren-Cosworth	lap 78	
7th	V.Elford	Cooper-Maserati	lap 74	

Fastest lap: P.Courage (Brabham-Cosworth V8), lap 57, 1 min. 25.8 131.958 k.p.h.

Retired: J.Oliver *(B.R.M. V12)*, lap 1, accident; J.Brabham *(Brabham-Cosworth V8)* lap 10, accident; J.Surtees *(B.R.M. V12)* lap 10, gearbox and accident; P.Rodriguez *(B.R.M. V12)* lap 16, engine; S.Moser *(Brabham-Cosworth V8)*, lap 16, drive-shaft universal; C.Amon *(Ferrari V12)* lap 17, differential; J-P.Beltoise *(Matra-Cosworth V8)*, lap 22, drive-shaft; J.Stewart *(Matra-Cosworth V8)* lap 23, drive-shaft; J.Ickx *(Brabham-Cosworth V8)*, lap 49, broken rear hub carrier.

The rules of Grand Prix motor racing have always been complex and ever changing. Life is further complicated by local rules and Monaco is no exception when it comes to making life difficult. Having been through various qualifying formulae, the Monaco authorities seemed to have settled down in the previous years to a sixteen car field, with ten invited entries guaranteed starts, and the remainder to fight over the spare six places. This seemed to be a reasonably happy compromise since no system of priorities could be completely fair. Frequently drivers had failed to qualify with

ENTRIES

DRIVER	TEAM	CAR
G. Hill	Brooke Bond Oxo Racing	Lotus-Cosworth V8
J. Miles	Lotus	Lotus-Cosworth V8
J. Rindt	Lotus	Lotus-Cosworth V8
A. Soler Roig	Worldwide Racing	Lotus-Cosworth V8
J. Brabham	Brabham	Brabham-Cosworth V8
R. Stommelen	Auto Motor und Sport	Brabham-Cosworth V8
D. Bell	Wheatcroft Racing	Brabham-Cosworth V8
H. Pescarolo	Matra-Elf	Matra-Simca
J-P. Beltoise	Matra-Elf	Matra-Simca
A. de Adamich	McLaren	McLaren-Alfa Romeo
D. Hulme	McLaren	McLaren-Cosworth V8
B. McLaren	McLaren	McLaren-Cosworth V8
J. Surtees	Surtees	McLaren-Cosworth V8
G. Eaton	B.R.M.	B.R.M. V12
J. Oliver	B.R.M.	B.R.M. V12
P. Rodriguez	B.R.M.	B.R.M. V12
J. Siffert	March	March-Cosworth V8
J. Servoz-Gavin	Tyrrell	March-Cosworth V8
J. Stewart	Tyrrell	March-Cosworth V8
M. Andretti	STP	March-Cosworth V8
R. Peterson	Antique Automobiles	March-Cosworth V8
P. Courage	Williams	De Tomaso-Cosworth
S. Moser	Moser	Bellasi-Cosworth V8
J. Ickx	Ferrari	Ferrari Flat-12
C. Amon	March	March-Cosworth V8

77

STARTING GRID

21	28
J. Stewart	**C. Amon**
1 min. 24.0	1 min. 24.6

11	5
D. Hulme	**J. Brabham**
1 min. 25.1	1 min. 25.4

26	8
J. Ickx	**J-P. Beltoise**
1 min. 25.5	1 min. 25.6

9	3
H. Pescarolo	**J. Rindt**
1 min. 25.7	1 min. 25.9

24	12
P. Courage	**B. McLaren**
1 min. 26.1	1 min. 26.1

19
J. Siffert
1 min. 26.2

23	14
R. Peterson	**J. Surtees**
1 min. 26.8	1 min. 27.4

16	17
J. Oliver	**P. Rodriguez**
1 min. 27.5	1 min. 28.8

1
G. Hill

times better than one of the guaranteed starters.

To start the '70s however, a new system was introduced. There were six available starting places and the competing drivers were given an extra half hour of practice to themselves on the Saturday. Any times recorded in that session could be used to qualify for the grid but would not place the driver in front of any guaranteed driver who happened to have a slower recorded time. Can you imagine translating that from the French?

Incidentally, while on the subject of rules - when is a lap record not a lap record? *When a driver does not complete the race.* Monaco rules again! In the 1969 race Stewart's lap in 1 min. 25.1 was not recorded as the lap record because of his subsequent retirement. Surely a lap time is a lap time whether the car does one lap or eighty? However, by the time the cars turned out for practice with a full knowledge of the rules, it was Stewart's lap that was in mind. Stewart himself in the March 701 Cosworth V8 and Amon also in a March 701 were very quickly off the mark with first day times below the lap record. Hulme in the McLaren M14A also went well early on. The B.R.M. mechanics were more than busy with their three cars (driven by Oliver, Rodriguez and Eaton).

The Friday session was ruined by continuous rain and nobody was prepared to take any risks. The period was mainly used by those working to get their cars running decently. Saturday at least was dry, and B.R.M.

finally got their act together to record respectable times, but were still at the back of the grid, only followed by Hill. Graham had shunted his Lotus in the last practice and was using a spare car for the race. Therefore his recorded times were not allowed.

Weather conditions improved for the start of the race and Stewart, who had dominated practice, led up the hill to Ste. Devote, with a following of Amon (March), Brabham (Brabham), Ickx (Ferrari), Beltoise (Matra), Hulme (McLaren), Rindt (Lotus), Pescarolo (Matra). Towards the end of lap one at the old Gasometer Hairpin, Beltoise outbraked Ickx to take fourth place. In fact, all of the leading group of eight cars were running well.

The procession continued for twelve laps with eight drivers tensely eyeing each other while waiting for someone to try something. That something proved to be the retirement of Ickx with a broken drive shaft. One lap later it was Surtees who retired to save a sickening engine.

Left
The Goodyear compound, just behind the swimming pool.

Jochen Rindt (Lotus 49 Cosworth V8)

The tense nose-to-tail - high speed chain continued its way for lap after lap, with Stewart extracting half second by half second a more comfortable lead from Amon. On lap 22 Brabham made a supreme effort to break the stalemate and forced his way past Amon. Within four more laps he was in the lead. The Scotsman suddenly slowed and turned into the pits with his engine firing only on a few of its eight cylinders. Though he was to rejoin the race later, he was unable to make any further challenge. So, as the leaders approached half way, the order was Brabham, Amon, Hulme, Pescarolo, Rindt, Siffert, Courage, Hill, Oliver, Peterson, Rodriguez and Stewart.

Amon's challenge to Brabham ended on lap 61 when his car's rear suspension came apart and gave him a fright. Hulme and Siffert were not running well and with Rindt apparently happy to sit in second place for the duration - Jack seemed to have the 1970 Monaco in his pocket and eased a little. Rindt, apparently without any particular effort on his own part finally spotted Brabham in front with only two laps left and realised he just might still have a chance.

Interesting comparison in front wing angles between Jack Brabham's car and Chris Amon's March.

A man of Jack Brabham's experience is very difficult to overtake around the streets, if he doesn't want to be overtaken. On the last bend of the last lap it looked all over, but to the amazement of all, particularly Rindt, Brabham was on the wrong line due to a tail ender. He spun off into the barriers and Rindt duly drove across the line for his first Monaco win!

It is worthy of note that Rindt may have been a little lucky, but his last lap was a record 1 min. 23.3 and without that charge Brabham's win would have been a formality.

Above
Jack Brabham driving his own car to second place.

Below
Pescarolo in the Matra-Simca V12 finished third.

81

Above
Rindt braking very hard for the chicane.

Inset
An exuberant Jochen Rindt celebrates his first victory at Monaco.

TWENTY-EIGHTH
GRAND PRIX
OF MONACO
RESULTS

1st	J.Rindt	Lotus 49C	lap 80	1 hr. 54 min. 36.6
2nd	J.Brabham	Brabham BT33	lap 80	1 hr. 54 min. 59.7
3rd	H.Pescarolo	Matra-Simca MS120	lap 80	1 hr. 55 min. 28.0
4th	D.Hulme	McLaren-M14A	lap 80	1 hr. 56 min. 04.9
5th	G.Hill	Lotus 49C	lap 79	
6th	P.Rodriguez	B.R.M. 153	lap 78	
7th	R.Peterson	March 701	lap 78	
8th	J.Siffert	March 701	lap 76	
9th	P.Courage	De Tomaso 38	lap 56	

Fastest lap: J.Rindt (Lotus 49C/R6), lap 80, 1 min. 23.2 136.081 k.p.h. *(new record)*

Retired: J.Ickx *(Ferrari 312B/001)*, lap 12, drive shaft; J.Surtees *(McLaren M7C/1)*, lap 15, low oil pressure; B.McLaren *(McLaren M14A/1)*, lap 20, damaged suspension; J-P.Beltoise *(Matra-Simca MS120/01)*, lap 23, transmission, J.Oliver *(B.R.M. 153/04)*, lap 43, engine; J.Stewart *(March 701/2)*, lap 57, engine, C.Amon *(March 701/1)*, lap 61, suspension.

After the complexities of qualifying for the 1970 race, some simple minded soul suggested that they let the fastest drivers make up the starting grid and forget all about guaranteed starts. The Automobile Club of Monaco said "... why didn't we think of that?", and the proposal was adopted. Eighteen cars were allowed to start instead of the usual sixteen, which made the major teams reasonably happy.

The first day of practice was virtually rained off, conditions being so bad that only a few cars ventured out, and little was achieved. Many of the teams had brand new models to try out, and needed as much circuit

ENTRIES

DRIVER	TEAM	CAR
E. Fittipaldi	Lotus	Lotus-Cosworth V8
R. Wisell	Lotus	Lotus-Cosworth V8
J. Ickx	Ferrari	Ferrari-Flat 12
G. Regazzoni	Ferrari	Ferrari-Flat 12
M. Andretti	Ferrari	Ferrari-Flat 12
G. Hill	Brabham	Brabham-Cosworth V8
T. Schenken	Brabham	Brabham-Cosworth V8
D. Hulme	McLaren	McLaren-Cosworth V8
P. Gethin	McLaren	McLaren-Cosworth V8
J. Stewart	Tyrrell	Tyrrell-Cosworth V8
F. Cevert	Tyrrell	Tyrrell-Cosworth V8
J. Siffert	B.R.M.	B.R.M.-V12
P. Rodriguez	B.R.M.	B.R.M.-V12
H. Ganley	B.R.M.	B.R.M.-V12
R. Peterson	March	March-Cosworth V8
A. Soler-Roig	March	March-Cosworth V8
N. Galli	March	March-Alfa Romeo V8
C. Amon	Matra	Matra-Simca V12
J-P. Beltoise	Matra	Matra-Simca V12
J. Surtees	Surtees	Surtees-Cosworth V8
R. Stommelen	Surtees	Surtees-Cosworth V8
H. Pescarolo	March	March-Cosworth V8
S. Barber	March	March-Cosworth V8

STARTING GRID

4 **J. Ickx** 1 min. 24.4	**11** **J. Stewart** 1 min. 23.2
20 **C. Amon** 1 min. 24.8	**14** **J. Siffert** 1 min. 24.8
9 **D. Hulme** 1 min. 25.3	**15** **P. Rodriguez** 1 min. 25.1
17 **R. Peterson** 1 min. 25.8	**21** **J-P. Beltoise** 1 min. 25.6
22 **J. Surtees** 1 min. 26.0	**7** **G. Hill** 1 min. 26.0
2 **R. Wisell** 1 min. 26.7	**5** **G. Regazzoni** 1 min. 26.1
10 **P. Gethin** 1 min. 26.9	**27** **H. Pescarolo** 1 min. 26.7
24 **R. Stommelen** 1 min. 27.2	**12** **F. Cevert** 1 min. 27.2
8 **T. Schenken** 1 min. 28.3	**1** **E. Fittipaldi** 1 min. 27.7

time as possible to set them up for the unique conditions of the Monaco streets.

The second session started dry but with a possibility of rain later, everyone was anxious to record a time early on resulting in congestion and frustration. Stewart was in fine form recording 1 min. 23.2 which the others were unable to match. Ickx, Amon and Siffert were also competitive, but clearly most of the teams, needed more preparation time. Unfortunately for them, the Saturday practice was also spoiled by wet conditions and so most had to settle for their Friday times.

Race day was dry and sunny, at least to begin with, but the prognosis was uncertain, as was the performance of a great many of the starters. Louis Chiron was once again to start the race to celebrate the 40th anniversary of his Monaco victory and after much elaborate flag waving, everyone managed to get away without mowing him down! Stewart led, with Siffert and Ickx following.

The first casualty was Hill who made one of his few errors at Monaco, to wreck the Brabham on the Armco barrier at Tabac. Meanwhile, Stewart, with absolute confidence in his Tyrrell, was storming away from everyone. This was to be his first World Championship year and he was displaying his driving virtuosity and superiority on probably the most difficult circuit in the world.

The Tyrrell - Cosworth V8 we must remember was not particularly superior to its rivals. This was the time of the 'kit-car' built around the legendary Ford-Cosworth engine, and though undoubtedly his car was truly on song at Monaco, only Stewart of the current Grand Prix drivers could display this level of domination. By half distance he had recorded a new lap record of 1 min. 23 and in the second half of the race he repeatedly set new best times.

Siffert held second place and bravely held on to the leader as best he could. Ickx in the Ferrari was a distant third and Peterson fourth. Schenken hit the kerb at the Gasworks Hairpin and pitted for two new wheels. Cevert in the second Tyrrell retired after bending his car.

At quarter distance the order was Stewart (Tyrrell), Siffert (B.R.M.), Ickx (Ferrari), Peterson (March), Hulme (McLaren), Beltoise (Matra), Wisell (Lotus), Pescarolo (March), Regazzoni (Ferrari), Stommelen (Surtees), Fittipaldi (Lotus), Surtees (Surtees), and Gethin (McLaren).

Regazzoni was the next victim of the Monaco kerb stones, requiring two new wheels and Wisell retired pro-

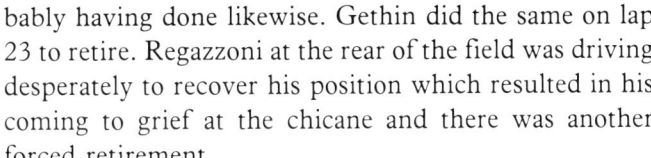

bably having done likewise. Gethin did the same on lap 23 to retire. Regazzoni at the rear of the field was driving desperately to recover his position which resulted in his coming to grief at the chicane and there was another forced retirement.

The winner - Jackie Stewart - Tyrrell Cosworth V8.

Stewart's driving was too perfect to be exciting, but all attention was on Peterson when he overtook both Ickx and Siffert to claim second place. Grand Prix enthusiasts were accustomed to his exuberant driving but he was undoubtedly very skilful and did not touch those lethal kerb stones. All his efforts, however, made no impression on the leader who was steadily extending his lead second upon second.

At lap 48 there were only four cars on the same lap as the leader - Peterson, Siffert, Ickx and Hulme. Of these Siffert lost his oil and retired. Stewart duly completed the 80 laps of his perfect race to receive the winner's accolade from Prince Rainier.

TWENTY-NINETH
GRAND PRIX
OF MONACO
RESULTS

1st	J.Stewart	Tyrrell 003	lap 80	1 hr. 52 min. 21.3
2nd	R.Peterson	March 711/2	lap 80	1 hr. 52min. 46.9
3rd	J.Ickx	Ferrari 312B	lap 80	1 hr. 53 min. 14.6
4th	D.Hulme	McLaren M19	lap 80	1 hr. 53 min. 28.0
5th	E.Fittipaldi	Lotus 72D/R5	lap 79	
6th	R.Stommelen	Surtees TS9	lap 79	
7th	J.Surtees	Surtees TS9	lap 79	
8th	H.Pescarolo	March 711	lap 77	
9th	P.Rodriguez	B.R.M. P160	lap 76	
10th	T.Schenken	Brabham BT33	lap 76	

Fastest lap: J.Stewart (Tyrrell 003), lap 57, 1 min. 22.2, 137.737 k.p.h. *(new record)*

Retired: G.Hill*(Brabham BT34/1), lap 2, accident; F.Cevert (Tyrrell 002)* lap 6, accident; R.Wisell *(Lotus 72C/R3), lap 22, accident; P.Gethin (McLaren M14A/2) lap 23, accident; G.Regazzoni (Ferrari 312B/2-5), lap 25, accident; C.Amon (Matra-Simca MS120B/04), lap 46, transmission; J-P.Beltoise (Matra-Simca MS120B/05), lap 48, transmission; J.Siffert (B.R.M. P160/02) lap 59, oil pressure.*

Major changes had been made to the old Monaco circuit for the race of 1972. The pits, which had been in the
central area behind the Gasworks Hairpin, adjacent to
the start/finish line, had been moved to the stretch of
road after the chicane. The left turn into the chicane was
now the entrance to the pits, while the track now carried
straight on down what was the escape road to a new
chicane further along the quayside. Exit from the pits -
being completely blind for the drivers - was controlled
by a good old fashioned traffic light - hand controlled of
course. The result was much more working room for the
mechanics though there was little spectating facilities in
this area. There was little doubt that the changes were an
improvement.

ENTRIES

DRIVER	TEAM	CAR
J. Stewart	Tyrrell	Tyrrell-Cosworth V8
F. Cevert	Tyrrell	Tyrrell-Cosworth V8
R. Peterson	March	March-Cosworth V8
N. Lauda	March	March-Cosworth V8
M. Beuttler	March	March-Cosworth V8
J. Ickx	Ferrari	Ferrari-Flat 12
G. Regazzoni	Ferrari	Ferrari-Flat 12
E. Fittipaldi	Lotus	Lotus-Cosworth V8
D Walker	Lotus	Lotus-Cosworth V8
T. Schenken	Surtees	Surtees-Cosworth V8
M. Hailwood	Surtees	Surtees-Cosworth V8
A. de Adamich	Surtees	Surtees-Cosworth V8
D. Hulme	McLaren	McLaren-Cosworth V8
B. Redman	McLaren	McLaren-Cosworth V8
C. Amon	Matra	Matra-Simca V12
J-P. Beltoise	B.R.M.	B.R.M. V12
P. Gethin	B.R.M.	B.R.M. V12
H. Ganley	B.R.M.	B.R.M. V12
G. Hill	Brabham	Brabham-Cosworth V8
W. Fittipaldi	Brabham	Brabham-Cosworth V8
H. Pescarolo	Williams	March-Cosworth V8
C. Pace	Williams	March-Cosworth V8
R. Stommelen	Eifelland	Eifelland-Cosworth V8
R. Wisell	B.R.M.	B.R.M. V12

STARTING GRID

8 **E. Fittipaldi** 1 min. 21.4		**6** **J. Ickx** 1 min. 21.6
	7 **G. Regazzoni** 1 min. 21.9	**17** **J-P. Beltoise** 1 min. 22.5
18 **P. Gethin** 1 min. 22.6		**16** **C. Amon** 1 min. 22.6
	14 **D. Hulme** 1 min. 22.7	**1** **J. Stewart** 1 min. 22.9
22 **H. Pescarolo** 1 min. 22.9		**15** **B. Redman** 1 min. 23.1
	11 **M. Hailwood** 1 min. 23.7	**2** **F. Cevert** 1 min. 23.8
10 **T. Schenken** 1 min. 23.9		**9** **D. Walker** 1 min. 24.0
	3 **R. Peterson** 1 min. 24.1	**28** **R. Wisell** 1 min. 24.4
26 **H. Marko** 1 min. 24.6		**12** **A. de Adamich** 1 min. 24.7
	20 **G. Hill** 1 min. 24.7	**19** **H. Ganley** 1 min. 24.7
21 **W. Fittipaldi** 1 min. 25.2		**4** **N. Lauda** 1 min. 25.6
	5 **M. Beuttler** 1 min. 26.5	**23** **C. Pace** 1 min. 26.6
27 **R. Stommelen** 1 min. 29.5		

Not universally approved, however, was the decision to allow 25 cars to start which many thought would be too much traffic on the 1.9 mile circuit. Since there were just 25 drivers entered, there would be no elimination contest in practice.

When we recall the perfection of Jackie Stewart's 1971 lap record of 1 min. 22.2 it is difficult to believe that after seven years of the 3-litre formula, there was still room for improvement. Surely twelve months later, the cars would be pretty well the same? Yet practice, in similar dull, dry conditions, revealed that the leading cars were up to a second faster. The significant point to observe was that these were V 12 engined cars. The Ferraris of Ickx and Regazzoni, the B.R.M.s of Beltoise and Gethin and Amon's Matra. Only Fittipaldi in the Lotus was better than Stewart's time with the Cosworth engine. Could it be that the famous V8 was showing signs of age?

Sunday May 14th, rain and more rain, and yet the race duly started on time with all the cars wearing the deepest cut of wet weather tyres, and red tail lights like any common or garden Mini! It became apparent immediately how essential these were when the 25 cars 'streamed' away in a cloud of spray. Surely only the front rank could have seen where they were going and the rest just followed the red light in front! Beltoise and Ickx were the lucky two, and the B.R.M. driver made the most of his opportunity, very quickly opening up a commanding lead, after a good start from the second row. Regazzoni and Fittipaldi sorted themselves out from Ickx and settled down in that order. Amon, Stewart, Gethin, Redman and Hulme were just identifiable in the mist of spray. The pattern of things to come showed itself when Regazzoni over cooked it at the new chicane, took to the escape road and found Fittipaldi, following his red light, was still tight on his tail! This was not a race, it was a question of survival. If Beltoise stayed on the course, he would win, since any sort of overtaking manoeuvre was really out of the question except for the most foolhardy. The speed, of course, was pedestrian -an average of about 60 m.p.h. for the leader, and much lower for the rest, therefore the machinery was not under stress. Spins and escapes up slip roads were too numerous to record but amazingly there were no major crashes.

The half way positions were: Beltoise (B.R.M.), Ickx (Ferrari), Regazzoni (Ferrari), Stewart (Tyrrell), with the rest, 22 in all, in a constantly reshuffling confusion of

CIRCUIT

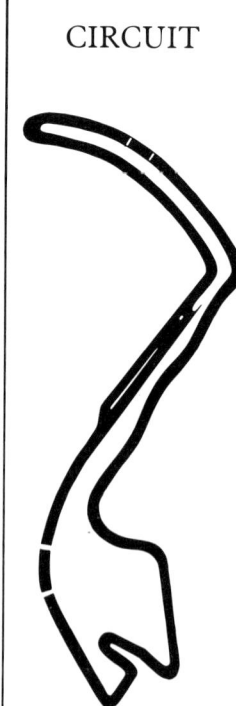

Above
Emerson Fittipaldi was happy to finish third in the Lotus 72.

Left
In the conditions overtaking required a certain amount of co-operation. Regazzoni (7) slips by Wilson Fittipaldi (21).

Below
Beltoise in control - in the wet.

Beltoise (B.R.M. P160-V12). Clearly visible are the air intakes to the front disc brakes.

cars! Stewart, for a period drove brilliantly and looked likely to move up to second from his fourth place, but a wild spin slowed down his efforts. Ganley (B.R.M.) shunted Hailwood (Surtees) in the rear, at the approach to the Gasworks Hairpin resulting in both retiring. Newcomer Hailwood must have wished he had stuck to motorcycles! The resulting oily trail to Ste. Devote led to Regazzoni losing whatever control he had, and he smashed the Ferrari into the barriers.

Beltoise skated his precarious way around the streets and duly recorded his victory, but this really was more of a black comedy than a Grand Prix motor race. Though nobody would denigrate the skill of Beltoise in appalling conditions, this was not the grande épreuve that Monaco was accustomed to seeing.

THIRTIETH
GRAND PRIX
OF MONACO
RESULTS

1st	J-P. Beltoise	B.R.M. P160	lap 80	2 hr. 25 min. 54.7
2nd	J.Ickx	Ferrari 312B	lap 80	2 hr. 27 min. 32.9
3rd	E.Fittipaldi	Lotus 72D	lap 79	
4th	J.Stewart	Tyrrell 004	lap 78	
5th	B.Redman	McLaren M19A	lap 77	
6th	C.Amon	Matra-Simca MS120	lap 77	
7th	A.de Adamich	Surtees TS9B	lap 77	
8th	H.Marko	B.R.M. P153	lap 77	
9th	W.Fittipaldi	Brabham BT33	lap 77	
10th	R.Stommelen	Eifelland-March 721	lap 77	
11th	R.Peterson	March 721X	lap 76	
12th	G.Hill	Brabham BT37	lap 76	
13th	M.Beuttler	March 721G	lap 76	
14th	D.Walker	Lotus 72D	lap 75	
15th	D.Hulme	McLaren M19C	lap 74	
16th	N.Lauda	March 721X	lap 74	
17th	C.Pace	March 711	lap 72	
18th	F.Cevert	Tyrrell 002	lap 70	

Fastest lap:
J-P.Beltoise (B.R.M. P160) lap 9, 1 min. 40.0 113.220 k.p.h.

Ickx in the Ferrari was overtaken by Beltoise on the first corner and was never able to regain the lead.

Retired:
R.Wisell (B.R.M. P160/04), lap 16, engine;
P.Gethin (B.R.M. P160/03) lap 28, accident;
T.Schenken (Surtees TS9B/006), lap 32, accident;
H.Ganley (B.R.M. P180/02), lap 48, collision;
M.Hailwood (Surtees TS9B/005), lap 49, collision;
G.Regazzoni (Ferrari 312B2 No. 5), lap 52, accident;
H.Pescarolo (March 721/3), lap 58, accident

Changes to the circuit since the first race in 1929 had been few. The road surface had been improved over the years, particularly when the tram tracks had been removed in 1932. The line through various corners had been amended by the use of Armco fencing, but the old circuit had not been re-routed in any area. As mentioned in the previous chapter, the pits had been moved for the 1972 race to the area of the old chicane on Quai des Etats Unis. This was a constructive change since the old pits area between Quai Albert Premier and the Boulevard Albert Premier had always been too cramped and not altogether safe.

ENTRIES

DRIVER	TEAM	CAR
E. Fittipaldi	Lotus	Lotus-Cosworth V8
R. Peterson	Lotus	Lotus-Cosworth V8
J. Ickx	Ferrari	Ferrari-Flat 12
A. Merzario	Ferrari	Ferrari-Flat 12
J. Stewart	Tyrrell	Tyrrell-Cosworth V8
F. Cevert	Tyrrell	Tyrrell-Cosworth V8
D. Hulme	McLaren	McLaren-Cosworth V8
P. Revson	McLaren	McLaren-Cosworth V8
A. de Adamich	Brabham	Brabham-Cosworth V8
C. Reutemann	Brabham	Brabham-Cosworth V8
W. Fittipaldi	Brabham	Brabham-Cosworth V8
G. Hill	Hill	Shadow-Cosworth V8
J-P. Jarier	March	March-Cosworth V8
M. Beuttler	March	March-Cosworth V8
G. Follmer	U.O.P.-Shadow	Shadow-Cosworth V8
J. Oliver	U.O.P.-Shadow	Shadow-Cosworth V8
D. Purley	Purley	March-Cosworth V8
G. Regazzoni	B.R.M.	B.R.M.-V12
J-P. Beltoise	B.R.M.	B.R.M.-V12
N. Lauda	B.R.M.	B.R.M.-V12
C. Amon	Amon	Tecno-McCall-Flat 12
M. Hailwood	Surtees	Surtees-Cosworth V8
C. Pace	Surtees	Surtees-Cosworth V8
H. Ganley	Williams	Williams-Cosworth V8
N. Galli	Williams	Williams-Cosworth V8
J. Hunt	Hesketh	March-Cosworth V8

STARTING GRID

5 **J. Stewart** 1 min. 27.5	2 **R. Peterson** 1 min. 27.7
7 **D. Hulme** 1 min. 27.8	6 **F. Cevert** 1 min. 27.9
1 **E. Fittipaldi** 1 min. 28.1	21 **N. Lauda** 1 min. 28.5
3 **J. Ickx** 1 min. 28.7	19 **G. Regazzoni** 1 min. 28.9
11 **W. Fittipaldi** 1 min. 28.9	25 **H. Ganley** 1 min. 29.0
20 **J-P. Beltoise** 1 min. 29.0	22 **C. Amon** 1 min. 29.3
23 **M. Hailwood** 1 min. 29.4	14 **J-P. Jarier** 1 min. 29.4
8 **P. Revson** 1 min. 29.4	4 **A. Merzario** 1 min. 29.5
24 **C. Pace** 1 min. 29.6	27 **J. Hunt** 1 min. 29.9
10 **C. Reutemann** 1 min. 30.1	15 **M. Beuttler** 1 min. 31.0
26 **N. Galli** 1 min. 31.1	17 **J. Oliver** 1 min. 31.2
18 **D. Purley** 1 min. 31.9	12 **G. Hill** 1 min. 31.9

9
A. de Adamich
1 min. 32.1

Right
Stewart, having lapped his team mate Cevert, helped him to make up a number of places. Seen here driving down the hill from the Casino.

Only the unique character of the race and its setting had allowed the continuation of the race while the pits were in that situation.

The 1972 site for the pits had been popular with the Grand Prix circus but not with the viewing public, who were prepared to pay large sums of money for a view of the pit activity. Unfortunately, there was little room for viewing at the old chicane.

After the 1972 race there was major redevelopment of the Tir aux Pigeons tunnel area. The road from the Portier corner had been widened and an arcade covered the approach to the tunnel making the artificially lit area much longer. After the tunnel and the down hill stretch back to Quai level, the chicane had returned to its original site, and the circuit rejoined the Quai des Etats Unis as it had originally. A new harbour front road now turned left below the Tabac corner and circled the swimming pool on the harbour side before returning to the old circuit at the Gasworks Hairpin. The old road from Tabac to the Gasworks Hairpin was now the pits area, which was entered after the hairpin from Boulevard Albert Premier and exited near the start/finish line. The new road around the swimming pool would undoubtedly slow everyone down, since overtaking was virtually impossible in this area.

The 1972 practice had been a triumph for the V12 engined cars and it seemed possible that the Cosworth engine was reaching the end of its life. One year later the engine seemed to have received a new lease of life. Practice was dominated by the Tyrrell, Lotus and McLaren cars, which duly filled the first three rows of the starting grid, with only Niki Lauda in the B.R.M. V12 interfering with their monopoly. Pole position was achieved by Jackie Stewart once again with a time of 1 min. 27.5, which when compared with the old lap record of 1 min. 22.2, showed the effect of the circuit changes. Therefore it was decided that the race would be decided over 78 laps instead of 80, since Grand Prix regulations now stipulated that races should not extend for longer than two hours. It is interesting to remember that Stirling Moss drove for 2 hours 45 minutes when winning the race in 1961. But before we accuse the modern racing driver of being pampered, we must bear in mind that Bandini's fatal crash in 1967 was attributed to driver fatigue.

In contrast to the previous year, the start was blessed with glorious sunny weather. Cevert in the Tyrrell made a brilliant start from the second row to lead Peterson into

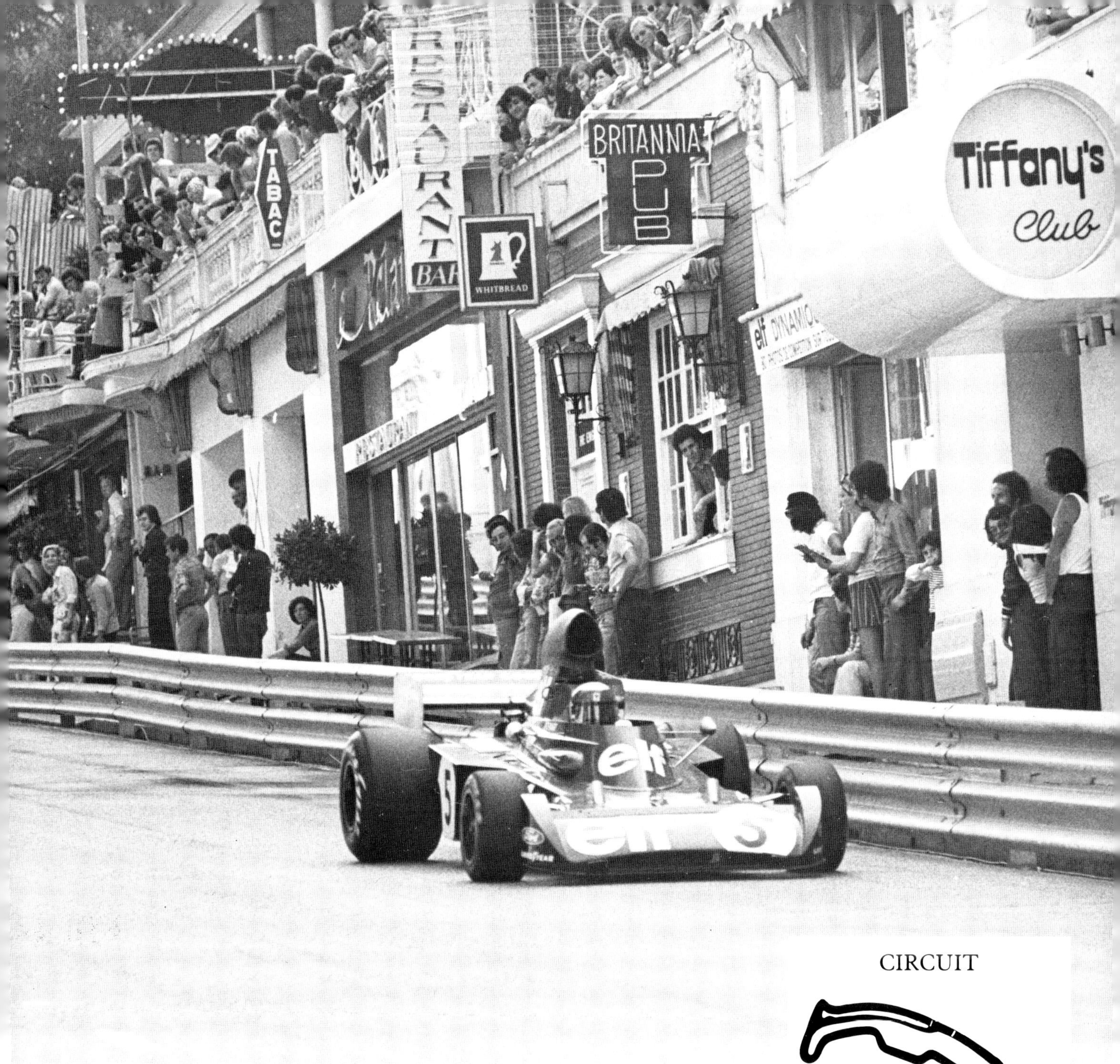

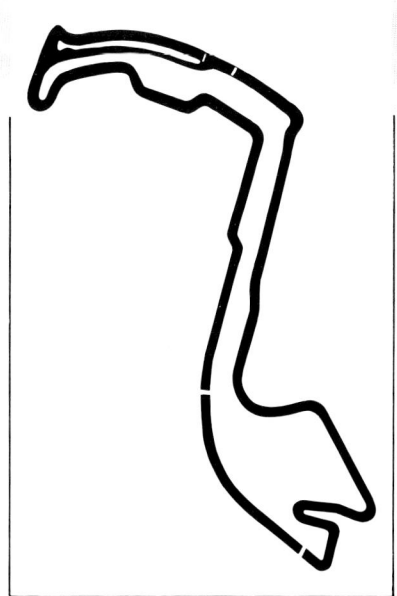

CIRCUIT

Ste. Devote. Regazzoni was also very quick off the mark and was ahead of Stewart. The Tyrrell lead was short lived however as an early puncture sent Cevert back to the pits, leaving Peterson in the lead. Regazzoni was unable to keep with the Lotus and in fact was holding up the rest of the field, while Peterson extended his lead.

Fortunately for Stewart and the others, Regazzoni returned to the pits after five laps, with brake problems. Meanwhile Peterson had a drop in power and was coming back to Stewart and Fittipaldi. Stewart took the lead on lap 8 and Fittipaldi followed him past Peterson into second place. One lap later and the ailing Lotus had dropped back to sixth place and was still losing ground.

The leaders settled into a steady pace, burning away

93

Above
Ronnie Peterson takes the beautiful Lotus 72 on a tight line at Portier.

Top right
Emerson Fittipaldi throwing the Lotus through a bend - definitely on ten-tenths!

Right
The Tyrrell Cosworth V8 in the hands of the winner - Jackie Stewart.

the laps, each warily watching the others. Amon dropped out with a puncture, to rejoin later at the rear of the field, but most interest centred on Cevert who was carving his way through the tail enders. The leaders were: Stewart (Tyrrell), E.Fittipaldi (Lotus), Lauda (B.R.M.), Ickx (Ferrari), W.Fittipaldi(Brabham), Peterson (Lotus), Ganley (Williams), Hulme (McLaren), Hailwood (Surtees), Pace (Surtees), Jarier (March).

On lap 25 Lauda retired the B.R.M. with a broken gear box, but the leaders - Stewart and Fittipaldi were well clear of the rest, with the Lotus applying constant pressure to the Tyrrell. Stewart was well into lapping the tail enders, and when he passed his team mate Cevert, now in 15th place, Cevert tucked into his slip stream and Stewart helped him past Revson, Merzario and Hunt.

On lap 40 Beltoise in the B.R.M. lost his way in Casino Square and demolished his car on the Armco while descending the steep hill down to Mirabeau. Ickx was the next to go with a broken drive shaft and then Ganley with a similar problem. The order was now Stewart, E.Fittipaldi, W.Fittipaldi, Hulme, Cevert. Cevert was still tailing Stewart, though a lap behind, and was still ahead of Emerson Fittipaldi on the road.

94

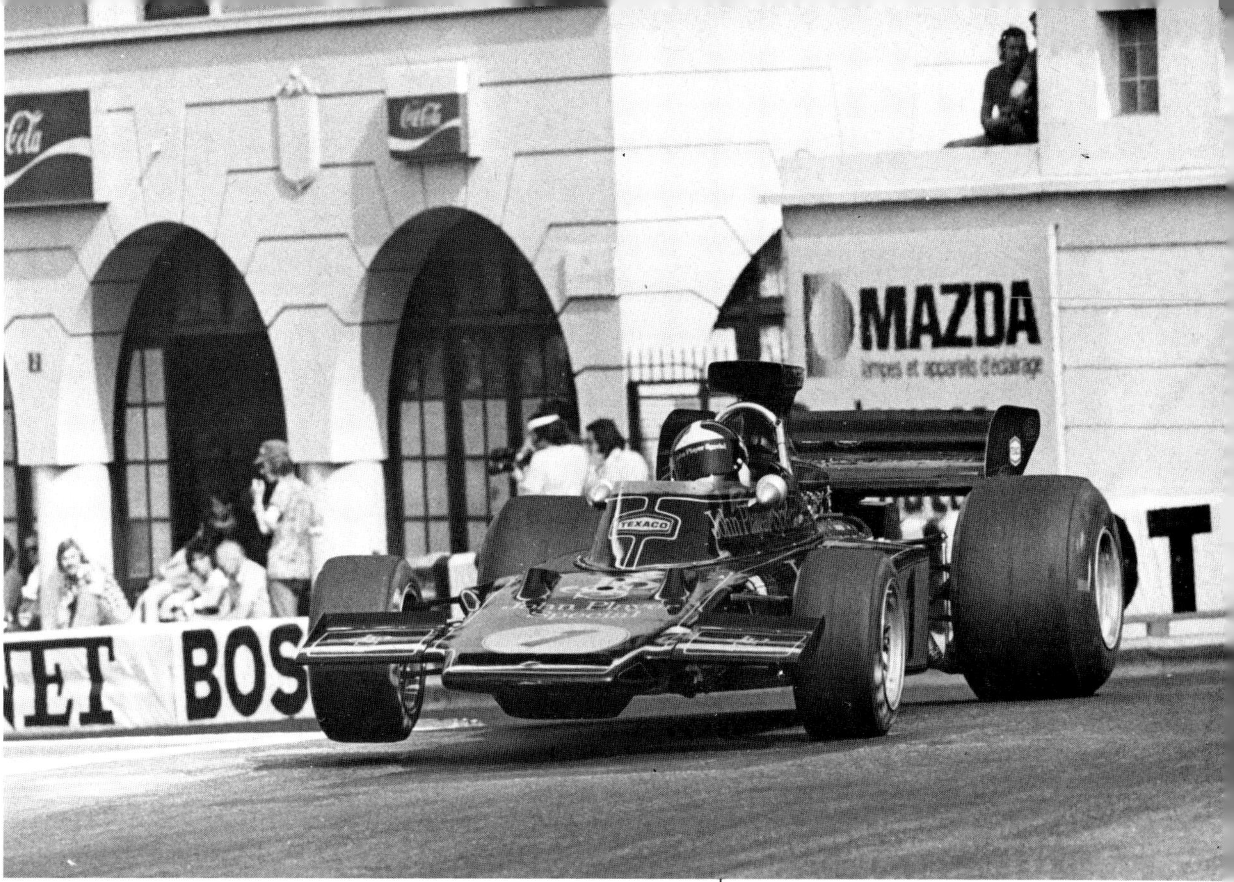
MAZDA
TEXACO
BOS

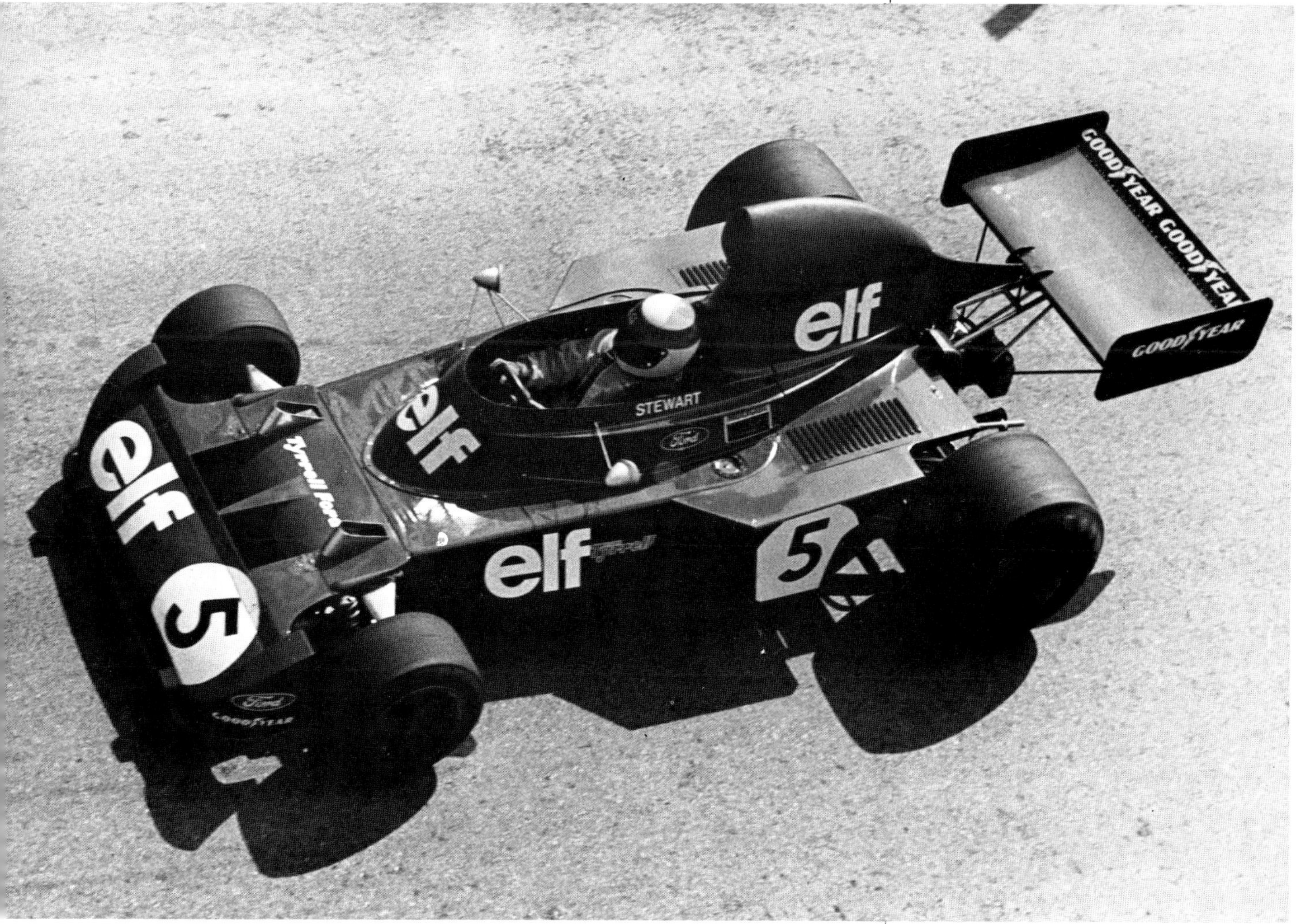
GOODYEAR
elf
STEWART
5

THIRTY - FIRST
G R A N D P R I X
O F M O N A C O
R E S U L T S

The closing laps were enlivened by Fittipaldi in the Lotus as he made one last great effort to catch Stewart. Cevert of course was in the ideal position to bulk the Lotus and protect his team mate, but sportingly he moved aside to allow the second place man to make his effort. Stewart however required no help and, though Fittipaldi closed to within a couple of seconds, the Tyrrell driver took the chequered flag to win his third Monaco Grand Prix.

1st	J.Stewart	Tyrrell 006	lap 78	1 hr. 57 min. 44.3
2nd	E.Fittipaldi	Lotus 72/R7	lap 78	1 hr. 57 min. 45.6
3rd	R.Peterson	Lotus 72/R6	lap 77	
4th	F.Cevert	Tyrrell 006	lap 77	
5th	P.Revson	McLaren M23	lap 76	
6th	D.Hulme	McLaren M23	lap 76	
7th	A.de Adamich	Brabham BT37/2	lap 75	
8th	M.Hailwood	Surtees TS14A	lap 75	
9th	J.Hunt	March 731/1	lap 73	
10th	J.Oliver	Shadow DN1/4A	lap 72	

Fastest lap: E.Fittipaldi (Lotus 72/R7), lap 78, 1 min. 28.1 133.947 k.p.h. *(record for new circuit)*

Retired: M.Beuttler *(March 721G/2)*, lap 3, engine; G.Regazzoni *(B.R.M. P160/07)*, lap 16, brakes; C.Amon *(Tecno PA123/6)*, lap 25, brakes and chassis; N.Lauda *(B.R.M. P160/08)*, lap 25, gearbox; N.Galli *(Williams IR/01)*, lap 31, drive-shaft universal; C.Pace *(Surtees TS14A/05)*, lap 31, drive-shaft; D.Purley *(March 731/3)*, lap 32, split fuel collector tank; J-P.Beltoise *(B.R.M. P160/03)* lap 40, accident at Mirabeau; H.Ganley *(Williams IR/02)*, lap 42, drive-shaft universal; J.Ickx *(Ferrari 312 B3/010)*, lap 45, rear driveshaft; C.Reutemann *(Brabham BT42/3)*, lap 47, gearbox; A.Merzario *(Ferrari 312 B3/011)*, lap 59, low oil pressure; G.Hill *(Shadow DN1/3A)*, lap 63, broken suspension mounting; J-P.Jarier *(March 721G/4)*, lap 68, gearbox; W.Fittipaldi *(Brabham BT42/3)*, lap 72, fuel system.

'74

A WIN FOR LOTUS

After the considerable upheaval of the reconstruction at Monaco in the previous two years, everyone breathed a sigh of relief when they arrived to find that no further alterations had been made. In fact life had been made a little easier by bevelling some of the more severe kerb stones. There had been a great many cars disabled by the kerbs in the previous two races, which had to be put down to the increasing performance of the grand prix machinery. The kerbs were certainly no worse than they had ever been but the G.P. car was now rather wider than before the 3-litre formula.

ENTRIES

DRIVER	TEAM	CAR
R. Peterson	Lotus	Lotus-Cosworth V8
J. Ickx	Lotus	Lotus-Cosworth V8
J. Scheckter	Tyrrell	Tyrrell-Cosworth V8
P. Depaillier	Tyrrell	Tyrrell-Cosworth V8
E. Fittipaldi	McLaren	McLaren-Cosworth V8
D. Hulme	McLaren	McLaren-Cosworth V8
C. Reutemann	Brabham	Brabham-Cosworth V8
R. von Opel	Brabham	Brabham-Cosworth V8
H-J. Stuck	March	March-Cosworth V8
V. Brambilla	March	March-Cosworth V8
G. Regazzoni	Ferrari	Ferrari-Flat 12
N. Lauda	Ferrari	Ferrari-Flat 12
J. P. Beltoise	B.R.M.	B.R.M. V12
H. Pescarolo	B.R.M.	B.R.M. V12
B. Redman	U.O.P.-Shadow	Shadow-Cosworth V8
J-P. Jarier	Shadow	Shadow-Cosworth V8
C. Pace	Surtees	Surtees-Cosworth V8
J. Mass	Surtees	Surtees-Cosworth V8
A. Merzario	Williams	Williams-Cosworth V8
V. Schuppan	Schuppan	Ensign-Cosworth V8
T. Schenken	Schenken	Trojan-Cosworth V8
J. Hunt	Hesketh	Hesketh-Cosworth V8
G. Hill	Lola	Lola-Cosworth V8
G. Edwards	Lola	Lola-Cosworth V8
J. Watson	Watson	Brabham-Cosworth V8
C. Amon	Amon	Amon-Cosworth V8
M. Hailwood	McLaren	McLaren-Cosworth V8
F. Migault	Migault	B.R.M. V12

STARTING GRID

12	11
N. Lauda	**G. Regazzoni**
1 min. 26.3	1 min. 26.6

1
R. Peterson
1 min. 26.8

3	17
J. Scheckter	**J-P. Jarier**
1 min. 27.1	1 min. 27.5

24	7
J. Hunt	**C. Reutemann**
1 min. 27.8	1 min. 27.8

9	33
H.-J. Stuck	**M. Hailwood**
1 min. 28.0	1 min. 28.1

14	6
J-P. Beltoise	**D. Hulme**
1 min. 28.1	1 min. 28.2

5	20
E. Fittipaldi	**A. Merzario**
1 min. 28.2	1 min. 28.5

10	16
V. Brambilla	**B. Redman**
1 min. 28.7	1 min. 28.8

2	18
J. Ickx	**C. Pace**
1 min. 29.4	1 min. 29.1

37	26
F. Migault	**G. Hill**
1 min. 30.0	1 min. 30.0

23	28
T. Schenken	**J. Watson**
1 min. 30.2	1 min. 30.0

27	22
G. Edwards	**V. Schuppan**
1 min. 30.4	1 min. 30.3

4T	15
P. Depailler	**H. Pescarolo**
1 min. 27.1	1 min. 30.7

This, combined with greater speed had reduced the margin for error considerably.

Once again 25 cars were to be allowed on the grid for the 78 lap race and 28 drivers commenced practice on the Thursday. Lotus provided two of last year's Lotus 72-Cosworth V8 for Peterson and Ickx, the new Lotus 76 was available but really only for testing purposes. Tyrrell had 007-Cosworth V8s for Scheckter and Depailler; Emerson Fittipaldi and Hulme had McLaren M23-Cosworth V8s; Reutemann and von Opel the Brabham BT44 - Cosworth V8; Stuck and Brambillo the March 741-Cosworth V8s. Ferrari arrived in force with immaculate 312B - Flat 12s for Regazzoni and Lauda plus a spare car and later in practice a second 'spare', indicating the seriousness of their effort. Beltoise and Pescarolo had the new B.R.M. P201-V12 and the old P160-V12 as their 'banker'. The Shadow DN3-Cosworth V8s were for Redman and Jarier; while John Surtees put his faith in Pace and Mass in Surtees TS16 - Cosworth V8s; Williams had just the one car for Merzario - the Williams IR-Cosworth V8; and there were single car entries for Schuppan -Ensign MN02 - Cosworth V8; Schenken -Trojan T103-Cosworth V8; Hunt -Hesketh 308 - Cosworth V8; Hill -Lola T370-Cosworth V8; Edwards -Lola T370-Cosworth V8; Watson -Brabham BT42-Cosworth V8; Amon -Amon AF101-Cosworth V8; Hailwood -McLaren M23-Cosworth V8; and Migault -B.R.M. P160-V12.

Someone calculated the total value of the machinery on display at well over £1,000,000! Formula One motor racing was clearly in a very healthy state.

Practice confirmed most peoples' thoughts that Ferrari were very serious this time. Their last win had been in 1955, and Lauda and Regazzoni set out to rectify the situation. Lauda was fastest on the first day with 1 min.

28.4 before smashing his car into the barriers along Quai Albert Premier. Unperturbed, he was again fastest in the spare car with 1 min. 26.3, which gave him pole position on the grid. Regazzoni, meanwhile had steadily improved on each day to share the front row with him. Peterson ran them closest of all the opposition. His early years had gained him a reputation for ragged driving, particularly at Monaco. However, nobody could criticise his performance in 1974.

The 32nd running of the Monaco Grand Prix started in dry, very warm weather. Regazzoni outdragged Lauda from the line, while managing to prevent Peterson from squeezing through from the second row. The line into Ste. Devote corner is strictly for one car at

Lap one - Regazzoni, Lauda, Jarier, Peterson.

Top left
Fittipaldi in the McLaren M23 charging through the tunnel.

99

Above
**Regazzoni in the Ferrari at Mirabeau.
A crane stands ready to clear the track
if required.**

Right
**Jody Scheckter in the Tyrrell leads
Mike Hailwood - the ex motor cycle
champion.**

a time, and Hulme found himself out of line and with no
space to dodge into. The result was a coming together
with the Beltoise B.R.M. and the Armco barrier, proving the old saying '... two into Ste. Devote, won't go!'
The following cars suddenly found the road completely
blocked and could only stop as best they could, which
was in most cases against another car. The result was the
retirement of Hulme, Redman, Pace, Merzario,
Schenken and, of course, Beltoise. Fortunately the
leaders were well clear - Regazzoni leading Lauda, Jarier,
Peterson, Reutemann, Scheckter, Hunt and Hailwood
together, the rest of the remaining field well behind. The
Marshalls did their usual efficient job and the road was
clear enough 1 min. 30 seconds later for the leaders to
pass through Ste. Devote unhindered.

100

Round the swimming pool.

The two leading Ferraris were clearly not under any team orders to assist each other. There was no hint of Lauda attempting to slow the rest down while his team mate extended the lead. Peterson in the Lotus, passed Jarier in the Shadow and began to apply the utmost pressure onto Lauda. But his judgement was at fault on lap 6 when he spun at the Gasworks Hairpin. His car was hit by Reutemann who was forced to retire, while Peterson was able to continue in sixth place.

Peterson immediately set about recovering his place. It took until lap 19 before he was able to get by Scheckter. Three laps later his cause was helped when Regazzoni also spun at the Gasworks Hairpin. The new leader, Lauda, began to pull away from Jarier, who now had the busy Lotus threatening him. On lap 25 Peterson was by and in second place and Lauda's lead was reducing noticeably each time they came by. Six laps later the Ferrari engine faltered under the strain and Peterson was already in the lead when Lauda came to a standstill on the Quai.

Jarier takes his Shadow DN3 through the old chicane.

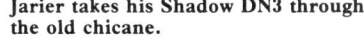

101

A subdued looking presentation group!

Right
The Lotus 72 clearly understeering its way through the hairpins.

THIRTY-SECOND
GRAND PRIX
OF MONACO
RESULTS

Meanwhile Scheckter had got by Jarier to hold second place in his first appearance at Monaco. The battle was over, since Scheckter was no match for the determined Peterson and in any case, well content to be in second place. The reliable old Lotus saw the leader through to the chequered flag and a memorable victory.

1st	R.Peterson	Lotus 72/R8	lap 78	1 hr. 58 min. 03.7
2nd	J.Scheckter	Tyrrell 007/1	lap 78	1 hr. 58 min. 32.5
3rd	J-P.Jarier	Shadow DN3/2A	lap 78	1 hr. 58 min. 52.6
4th	G.Regazzoni	Ferrari 312B3/014	lap 78	1 hr. 59 min. 06.8
5th	E.Fittipaldi	McLaren M23/5	lap 77	
6th	J.Watson	Brabham BT42/2	lap 77	
7th	G.Hill	Lola T370/HU2	lap 76	
8th	G.Edwards	Lola T370/HU1	lap 75	
9th	P.Depaillier	Tyrrell 006/2	lap 74	

Fastest Lap: R.Peterson (Lotus 72/R8) 1 min. 27.9 134.252 k.p.h.

Retired: D.Hulme *(McLaren M23/6)*, lap 1, accident; B.Redman *(Shadow DN3/3A)* lap 1 accident; C.Pace *(Surtees TS16/02)*, lap 1, accident; A.Merzario, *(Williams IR/04)*, lap 1, accident; T.Schenken *(Trojan T103)* lap 1, accident; J-P.Beltoise *(B.R.M. P201/01)* lap 1, accident; V.Brambilla *(March 741/2-2)*, lap 1, accident; H-J.Stuck *(March 741/1)* lap 3, accident; V.Schuppan *(Ensign MN02)* lap 5, accident; C.Reutemann *(Brabham BT44/3)* lap 6, accident; F.Migault *(B.R.M. P160/06)*, lap 9, accident; M.Hailwood *(McLaren M23/1)* lap 12, accident; J.Hunt *(Hesketh 308/2)* lap 28, drive shaft broke, N.Lauda *(Ferrari 312B3/010)* lap 33, ignition failure; J.Ickx *(Lotus 72/R5)* lap 34, engine broke; H.Pescarolo *(B.R.M. P160/10)* lap 63, gearbox broke.

Crashes prior to the 1975 race, plus the increasing performance of the Grand Prix car, had the whole motor racing world on edge. From time to time efforts are made to slow the cars down. New rules had been tried to make the engines smaller, or reduce the potency of the fuel, but no long term answer had ever been found. In each case the engineers and drivers had overcome their handicaps and eventually gone even faster. The introduction of Armco crash barriers helped to keep the spectators safe, but a car striking one tended to bounce around like a pea in a tin can, causing excessive damage to the car and even greater danger to the

ENTRIES

DRIVER	TEAM	CAR
E. Fittipaldi	McLaren	McLaren-Cosworth V8
J. Mass	McLaren	McLaren-Cosworth V8
J. Scheckter	Tyrrell	Tyrrell-Cosworth V8
P. Depailler	Tyrrell	Tyrrell-Cosworth V8
R. Peterson	Lotus	Lotus-Cosworth V8
J. Ickx	Lotus	Lotus-Cosworth V8
C. Reutemann	Brabham	Brabham-Cosworth V8
C. Pace	Brabham	Brabham-Cosworth V8
V. Brambilla	March	March-Cosworth V8
L. Lombardi	March	March-Cosworth V8
G. Regazzoni	Ferrari	Ferrari-Flat 12
N. Lauda	Ferrari	Ferrari-Flat 12
R. Evans	B.R.M.	B.R.M.-V12
T. Pryce	U.O.P.-Shadow	Shadow-Cosworth V8
J-P. Jarier	U.O.P.-Shadow	Shadow-Cosworth V8
J. Watson	Surtees	Surtees-Cosworth V8
A. Merzario	Williams	Williams-Cosworth V8
J. Laffite	Williams	Williams-Cosworth V8
G. Hill	Hill	Hill-Cosworth V8
J. Hunt	Hesketh	Hesketh-Cosworth V8
T. Palm	Hesketh	Hesketh-Cosworth V8
A. Jones	Hesketh	Hesketh-Cosworth V8
M. Andretti	Parnelli	Parnelli-Cosworth V8
M. Donohue	Penske	Penske-Cosworth V8
W. Fittipaldi	Fittipaldi	Fittipaldi-Cosworth V8
R. Wunderink	Wunderink	Ensign-Cosworth V8

STARTING GRID

12
N. Lauda
1 min. 26.40

16
T. Pryce
1 min. 27.09

17
J-P. Jarier
1 min. 27.25

5
R. Peterson
1 min. 27.40

9
V. Brambilla
1 min. 27.50

11
G. Regazzoni
1 min. 27.55

3
J. Scheckter
1 min. 27.58

8
C. Pace
1 min. 27.67

1
E. Fittipaldi
1 min. 27.77

7
C. Reutemann
1 min. 27.93

24
J. Hunt
1 min. 27.94

4
P. Depailler
1 min. 27.95

27
M. Andretti
1 min. 28.11

6
J. Ickx
1 min. 28.28

2
J. Mass
1 min. 28.49

28
M. Donohue
1 min. 28.81

18
J. Watson
1 min. 28.90

26
A. Jones
1 min. 29.12

other drivers. The Formula One cars were wider than ever before and at this time relatively equal in power, therefore overtaking was becoming increasingly hazardous. The rewards for success were very high as also was the investment in technology and as a result the pressure on the drivers to get results was even greater. Therefore in a situation where there is an entry of 26 drivers; a reduction to 18 places on the starting grid; a number of up and coming young drivers eager to prove themselves and to get on to the gravy train; the established circus of proven class drivers with their pride at stake; - it was inevitable that crashes would occur, particularly on the unforgiving circuit of Monaco.

Practice for the race had been reduced to only two sessions - on Thursday and Friday, with a rest day on Saturday and the race on the Sunday as usual.

As can be seen, the entry was full of Cosworth V8 'kit cars', with only Ferrari and B.R.M. still treading their own path. Even B.R.M. appeared to have lost faith, with only a token entry for Evans, a little known driver of limited ability. Fortunately, Ferrari were as strong and eager as ever. They had made a major effort at Monaco the previous year and only just failed. With two top class drivers they were again after that elusive win. Lauda and Regazzoni dominated the practice sessions, Regazzoni early on with 1 min. 27.7 and Lauda claiming pole position with a remarkable 1 min. 26.4, which had the timekeepers tapping their watches to see if they were working correctly! The V8s were not to be outdone though, and Pryce covered himself in glory with 1 min.27.09 and a place on the front row.

Perhaps nearly on the front row might be more correct because, for the first time at Monaco the cars were to line up in staggered pairs.

Above
Pace (Brabham BT44) and James Hunt (Hesketh 308).

Top left
Lauda, Peterson and Pryce in close company at the Upper Mirabeau.

The race was started in steady rain, with everyone on wet weather tyres, but with an optimistic forecast, there were mountains of 'slick' tyres ready and waiting in the pits. In clouds of spray, reminiscent of 1973, Lauda led the way up the hill to Ste. Devote, where recent improvements had reduced the road camber. In the first lap scramble both Regazzoni and Brambilla suffered minor damage to their cars, but were still mobile. As the cars emerged from the chicane for the first time Jarier made major modifications to his Shadow on the crash barriers and the car was swiftly hoisted out of the way. The early order was Lauda (Ferrari), Peterson (Lotus), Pryce (Shadow), Scheckter (Tyrrell), Fittipaldi (McLaren), Pace (Brabham), Hunt (Hesketh) and Depailler (Tyrrell).

105

Right
**Deep cut wet weather tyres very
apparent in this shot of Fittipaldi.**

Below
**Lauda leads in the early stages followed
by Jarier in the Shadow.**

The rain did not last long but the circuit was very
wet and slippery, and a change to dry weather tyres
would be probable at some stage of the race. The timing
of the change would very probably have a dramatic effect
on the result. The majority of the field settled down to
reeling off the laps, while remaining in contention until
the road dried out.

On lap 17 Hunt was the first one to make the decision to change. Mass was next and three laps later Pryce,
Pace and Watson followed suit. On lap 24 in came the
leaders - Lauda, Scheckter and Fittipaldi with Peterson a
lap later. So after the reshuffle the order was Lauda,
Depailler, Ickx, Fittipaldi, Scheckter, Pace. Depailler
and Ickx left their stops until lap 26 which dropped them
down the field and Peterson on rejoining the race had
dropped into fifth place.

The race settled down again with Fittipaldi, Pace,
Scheckter and Peterson content to follow Lauda.
Scheckter lost time and his place with a puncture and
Pryce went out after colliding with the barrier on the sea
front, spoiling an otherwise creditable performance.

It became evident after half way that the leaders had
lost too much time in the early part of the race to complete the full distance of 78 laps inside two hours.
Therefore, according to the F.I.A. rules the race ended
one lap after the time had elapsed, after, in fact 75 laps.
Ferrari had finally won for the first time since 1955 and
it was also a Monaco first for Lauda.

107

This year a happier looking prize-giving!

Right
Unusual shot of Niki Lauda and the Ferrari 312.

THIRTY-THIRD
GRAND PRIX
OF MONACO
RESULTS

1st	N.Lauda	Ferrari 312B3/023	lap 75	2 hr. 01 min. 21.31
2nd	E.Fittipaldi	McLaren M23/9	lap 75	2 hr. 01 min. 24.09
3rd	C.Pace	Brabham BT44B/2	lap 75	2 hr. 01 min. 39.12
4th	R.Peterson	Lotus 72/R9	lap 75	2 hr. 01 min. 59.76
5th	P.Depailler	Tyrrell 007/4	lap 75	2 hr. 02 min. 02.17
6th	J.Mass	McLaren M23/8	lap 75	2 hr. 02 min. 03.38
7th	J.Scheckter	Tyrrell 007/2	lap 74	
8th	J.Ickx	Lotus 72/R5	lap 74	
9th	C.Reutemann	Brabham BT44B/1	lap 73	

Fastest lap: P.Depailler (Tyrrell 007/4), lap 68, 1 min. 28.67 133.087 k.p.h.

Retired: J-P.Jarier *(Shadow DN5/21A)*, lap 1, accident; M.Andretti *(Parnelli VPJ4/003)*, lap 9, oil leak; G.Regazzoni *(Ferrari 312B3/018)* lap 37, accident; J.Watson *(Surtees TS16/02-4)*, lap 37, spun and no restart; T.Pryce *(Shadow DN5/2A)*, lap 38, accident; V.Brambilla *(March 751/3)* lap 50, damaged suspension; A.Jones *(Hesketh 308/1)* lap 62, wheel trouble; J.Hunt *(Hesketh 308/2)* lap 64, accident; M.Donohue *(Penske PC1/01-2)*, lap 67, accident

After a number of years of Cosworth 'kit cars' relieved by the occasional Ferrari flat-12 or B.R.M. V12, it was most interesting to see the new approach by Tyrrell at the 1976 Monaco Grand Prix. Two Project 34 cars were brought for Scheckter and Depailler. The P34 cars were six wheelers and there was immense interest, not only from the press and spectators, but also from the opposition teams. There are a great many teams who cannot afford the vast expense of experimenting with new concepts, for whom the 'kit car' era had been a great opportunity to compete at grand

ENTRIES

DRIVER	TEAM	CAR
N. Lauda	Ferrari	Ferrari-Flat 12
G. Regazzoni	Ferrari	Ferrari-Flat 12
J. Scheckter	Tyrrell	Tyrrell-Cosworth V8
P. Depailler	Tyrrell	Tyrrell-Cosworth V8
G. Nilsson	Lotus	Lotus-Cosworth V8
C. Reutemann	Brabham	Brabham-Alfa Romeo
C. Pace	Brabham	Brabham-Alfa Romeo
V. Brambilla	March	March-Cosworth V8
R. Peterson	March	March-Cosworth V8
J. Hunt	McLaren	McLaren-Cosworth V8
J. Mass	McLaren	McLaren-Cosworth V8
T. Pryce	U.O.P.-Shadow	Shadow-Cosworth V8
J-P. Jarier	U.O.P.-Shadow	Shadow-Cosworth V8
A. Jones	Surtees	Surtees-Cosworth V8
J. Ickx	Williams	Hesketh-Wlms.-Cos.
M. Leclere	Williams	Hesketh-Williams-Cosworth V8
C. Amon	Amon	Ensign-Cosworth V8
H. Ertl	Hesketh	Hesketh-Cosworth V8
J. Laffite	Ligier	Ligier-Matra V12
J. Watson	Penske	Penske-Cosworth V8
E. Fittipaldi	Fittipaldi	Fittipaldi-Cosworth V8
H-J. Stuck	March	March-Cosworth V8
A. Merzario	March	March-Cosworth V8
L. Perkins	Perkins	Ensign-Cosworth V8
H. Pescarolo	Pescarolo	Surtees-Cosworth V8

STARTING GRID

<table>
<tr><td></td><td>1
N. Lauda
1 min. 29.65</td></tr>
<tr><td>2
G. Regazzoni
1 min. 29.91</td><td></td></tr>
<tr><td></td><td>10
R. Peterson
1 min. 30.08</td></tr>
<tr><td>4
P. Depailler
1 min. 30.33</td><td></td></tr>
<tr><td></td><td>3
J. Scheckter
1 min. 30.55</td></tr>
<tr><td>34
H-J. Stuck
1 min. 30.60</td><td></td></tr>
<tr><td></td><td>30
E. Fittipaldi
1 min. 31.39</td></tr>
<tr><td>26
J. Laffite
1 min. 31.46</td><td></td></tr>
<tr><td></td><td>9
V. Brambilla
1 min. 31.47</td></tr>
<tr><td>17
J-P. Jarier
1 min. 31.65</td><td></td></tr>
<tr><td></td><td>12
J. Mass
1 min. 31.67</td></tr>
<tr><td>22
C. Amon
1 min. 31.75</td><td></td></tr>
<tr><td></td><td>8
C. Pace
1 min. 31.81</td></tr>
<tr><td>11
J. Hunt
1 min. 31.88</td><td></td></tr>
<tr><td></td><td>16
T. Pryce
1 min. 31.98</td></tr>
<tr><td>6
G. Nilsson
1 min. 32.10</td><td></td></tr>
<tr><td></td><td>28
J. Watson
1 min. 32.14</td></tr>
<tr><td>21
M. Leclere
1 min. 32.17</td><td></td></tr>
<tr><td></td><td>19
A. Jones
1 min. 32.33</td></tr>
<tr><td>7
C. Reutemann
1 min. 21.43</td><td></td></tr>
</table>

Top right
The four front wheels of the Tyrrell are tucked away into the bodywork as an aerodynamic improvement . Depailler driving.

Far right
Niki Lauda and the winning Ferrari emerge out of the gloom of the tunnel.

Right
The six wheel Tyrrell - seen here in practice near the swimming pool.

prix level. These teams can only watch developments introduced by the leading teams and copy. The two Tyrrell cars were still powered by the Cosworth V8, applying power through the rear wheels only, as usual, so the modification was clearly aimed to improve the handling. Depailler also had the old 007 four wheel car as a stand-by, but found it quite a handful, having got used to the new model.

Further minor modifications had been made to the circuit in the attempt to slow everyone down. A traffic island/chicane had been built at Ste. Devote. Of course it might even have been built for the benefit of the citizens of Monte Carlo, but the racing fraternity were convinced that it was a new chicane. Whatever the reason for its existence it was one more obstacle for the cars to run into and Brambilla duly obliged in the first session of practice. Spectators at the scene also scored near misses for Peterson, Jones and Jarier!

The Tyrrells took everyone by surprise by recording the best two times of the first session, and the press were immediately forecasting a design revolution and a complete grid of six-wheelers next time. The tyre manufacturers were also happy! World Champion Lauda swiftly calmed everyone down in the second session by recording a lap of nearly one second faster than the Tyrrells. Regazzoni and Peterson were also faster, but it was a most encouraging start for the new cars.

The race started at 3.30 p.m. on the Sunday from the 'staggered pairs' formation and for the first time the starting signal was given by coloured lights suspended over the road. Some thought the new system impersonal, but it had to be an improvement on Chiron and his flag!

The 'staggered pairs' formation seemed to take the excitement out of the start, but it had to be conceded that it got almost everyone through the Ste. Devote chicane, the victims being Reutemann and Jones. Lauda led from Peterson, Regazzoni and the two Tyrrells.

Lauda and the Ferrari seemed to be in a class of their own, quickly opening up a very large gap on the second place March. The driving of Peterson and Regazzoni

was wild in comparison, as they tried desperately to keep in touch. At one third distance the lead was a clear eight seconds, which, at Monaco, is out of sight!

Regazzoni had been trying desperately to get by Peterson, but lost his position when he skidded on oil at the old chicane. He restarted in fifth place. Three laps later Peterson crashed into the barrier at Tabac and was unable to continue. The order was Lauda (Ferrari), Scheckter (Tyrrell), Depailler (Tyrrell), Regazzoni (Ferrari), Laffite (Ligier), Fittipaldi (Fittipaldi), Stuck (March), Mass (McLaren), Jarier (Shadow), Pace (Brabham), Amon, Pryce, Nilsson, Watson and Leclere.

Meanwhile Depailler in the new Tyrrell obviously had a problem with a rear wheel tilted at an odd angle, but nevertheless he pressed on and was holding his place! Regazzoni would probably have the speed to pass him eventually. Incredibly it took until lap 64 for the Ferrari to get into third place, which Depailler accepted with good grace. Regazzoni was now intent on achieving a Ferrari 1/2 and chased desperately after Scheckter. The other healthy Tyrrell was a different proposition however, and Regazzoni eventually overdid things after the Tabac and rammed his Ferrari into the rail.

Lauda collected the winner's cup from Princess Grace for the second year in a row, and the Ferrari team were smiling again. Tyrrell were also hugely encouraged by the six-wheeler's performances.

THIRTY-FOURTH

GRAND PRIX
OF MONACO

RESULTS

1st	N.Lauda	Ferrari 312/023 (T4)	lap 75	2 hr. 01 min. 21.31
2nd	E.Fittipaldi	McLaren M23/9	lap 75	2 hr. 01 min. 24.09
3rd	C.Pace	Brabham BT44B/2	lap 75	2 hr. 01 min. 39.12
4th	R.Peterson	Lotus 72/R9	lap 75	2 hr. 01 min. 59.76
5th	P.Depailler	Tyrrell 007/4	lap 75	2 hr. 02 min. 02.17
6th	J.Mass	McLaren M23/8	lap 75	2 hr. 02 min. 03.38
7th	J.Scheckter	Tyrrell 007/2	lap 74	
8th	J.Ickx	Lotus 72/R5	lap 74	
9th	C.Reutemann	Brabham BT44B/1	lap 73	

Fastest lap: P.Depailler (Tyrrell 007/4), lap 68, 1 min. 28.67 133.087 k.p.h.

Retired: J.P.Jarier *(Shadow DN5/1A)*, lap 1, accident; M.Andretti *(Parnelli VPJ4/003)* lap 9, oil leak; G.Regazzoni *(Ferrari 312B3/018 (T1)*, lap 37, accident; J.Watson *(Surtees TS16/02-4)* lap 37, spun and no restart; T.Pryce *(Shadow DN5/2A)*, lap 38, accident; V.Brambilla *(March 751)*, lap 50, damaged suspension; A.Jones *(Hesketh 308/1)*, lap 62, wheel trouble; J.Hunt *(Hesketh 308/2)*, lap 64, accident; M.Donohue *(Penske PC1/01-2)*, lap 67, accident.

Although Monaco is far from the ideal venue for a Formula One Grand Prix race it has never failed to attract the best cars and drivers each time it has been held. Over the years the increasing performance of the cars had effectively made the circuit too narrow for reasonable overtaking, and with the circuit virtually fenced in by crash barriers, the chances of any competitive team going home unscathed was remote. The organisers had tried many ways to reduce the number of crashes and the 1977 amendment to the rules stated that there was to be no overtaking from the start to the Ste. Devote corner. The chances of 20 drivers, with

ENTRIES

DRIVER	TEAM	CAR
J. Hunt	McLaren	McLaren-Cosworth V8
J. Mass	McLaren	McLaren-Cosworth V8
R. Peterson	Tyrrell	Tyrrell-Cosworth V8
P. Depailler	Tyrrell	Tyrrell-Cosworth V8
M. Andretti	Lotus	Lotus 78-Cosworth V8
G. Nilsson	Lotus	Lotus-Cosworth V8
J. Watson	Brabham	Brabham-Alfa Romeo
H. Stuck	Brabham	Brabham-Alfa Romeo
A. Ribiero	A.T.S.	March-Cosworth V8
J. Scheckter	A.T.S.	March-Cosworth V8
N. Lauda	Ferrari	Ferrari-Flat 12
C. Reutemann	Ferrari	Ferrari-Flat 12
R. Patrese	A.V.S. Shadow	Shadow-Cosworth V8
A. Jones	A.V.S. Shadow	Shadow-Cosworth V8
H. Binder	Surtees	Surtees-Cosworth V8
V. Brambilla	Surtees	Surtees-Cosworth V8
J. Scheckter	Wolf	Wolf-Cosworth V8
G. Regazzoni	Wolf	Ensign-Cosworth V8
J. Ickx	Wolf	Ensign-Cosworth V8
R. Keegan	Hesketh	Hesketh-Cosworth V8
H. Ertl	Hesketh	Hesketh-Cosworth V8
J. Ligier	Hesketh	Ligier-Matra V12
E. Fittipaldi	Fittipaldi	Fittipaldi-Cosworth V8
B. Hayji	Hayji	March-Cosworth V8

Right
Jody Scheckter leads Watson's Brabham through Mirabeau.

Inset
Reutemann's Ferrari riding high over the brow of the hill.

Below
The business end of Scheckter's Wolf WR.

adrenalin flowing at the start of a major race, even remembering the rule, let alone obeying it, was unlikely!

So in spite of the expense and the petty-fogging rules, the grand prix circus seemed happy to once again pit their skills against the Monaco circuit. Twenty-six drivers were to compete in practice for twenty places on the grid, over three sessions - two on Thursday and one on Saturday.

Quickly into their stride at the beginning of Thursday's first session of practice, were Jody Scheckter and Ronnie Peterson. The six wheel Tyrrells which had been so successful at the 1976 race had been brought back for another try, in spite of disappointing performances in the last year. Watson and Stuck in the Brabhams were both enjoying themselves and Stuck recorded the best time in that session (1 min. 30.73). Making his first appearance in Formula One was Riccardo Patrese, driving a Shadow.

The second session in the afternoon was ruined by steady rain and few ventured out, except to test their wet weather gear. All that remained was the one hour session on the Saturday for those unable to get things right on Thursday. Fortunately for the strugglers there were withdrawals before then. Regazzoni decided his car had no chance, Ian Scheckter and Ribiero had both crashed their cars. So, in dry conditions once again everyone came out for their final one hour thrash.

114

The 1977 race was to be held over 76 laps of the 3.3 kilometre circuit, and once again the start was initiated by the traffic light system. Scheckter 'forgot' the new rule and overtook Watson before Ste. Devote, but it could be argued that he was on the front row of the grid, even if it was a staggered grid. Anyway the organisers turned a blind eye and no black flag was shown. Watson, annoyed at himself for his poor start had put the nose of his Brabham tight into the slip stream of the Wolf and was intent on making life uncomfortable for the leader. Reutemann, Stuck, Peterson, and Lauda were all going well and were in touch.

The six wheel Tyrrell was again proving unreliable. Peterson only lasted ten laps before retiring with brake problems and Depailler was having similar problems but kept going. Stuck also retired early on with an electrical problem that sparked off a major fire before he

STARTING GRID

7 **J. Watson** 1 min. 29.86	
	20 **J. Scheckter** 1 min. 30.27
12 **C. Reutemann** 1 min. 30.44	
	3 **R. Peterson** 1 min. 30.72
8 **H. J. Stuck** 1 min. 30.73	
	11 **N. Lauda** 1 min. 30.76
1 **J. Hunt** 1 min. 30.85	
	4 **P. Depailler** 1 min. 31.16
2 **J. Mass** 1 min. 31.36	
	5 **M. Andretti** 1 min. 31.50
17 **A. Jones** 1 min. 32.04	
	34 **J.P. Jarier** 1 min. 32.32
6 **G. Nilsson** 1 min. 32.37	
	19 **V. Brambilla** 1 min. 32.40
16 **R. Patrese** 1 min. 32.52	
	26 **J. Laffite** 1 min. 32.65
22 **J. Ickx** 1 min. 33.25	
	28 **E. Fittpaldi** 1 min. 33.39
18 **H. Binder** 1 min. 33.49	
	24 **R. Keegan** 1 min. 33.78

115

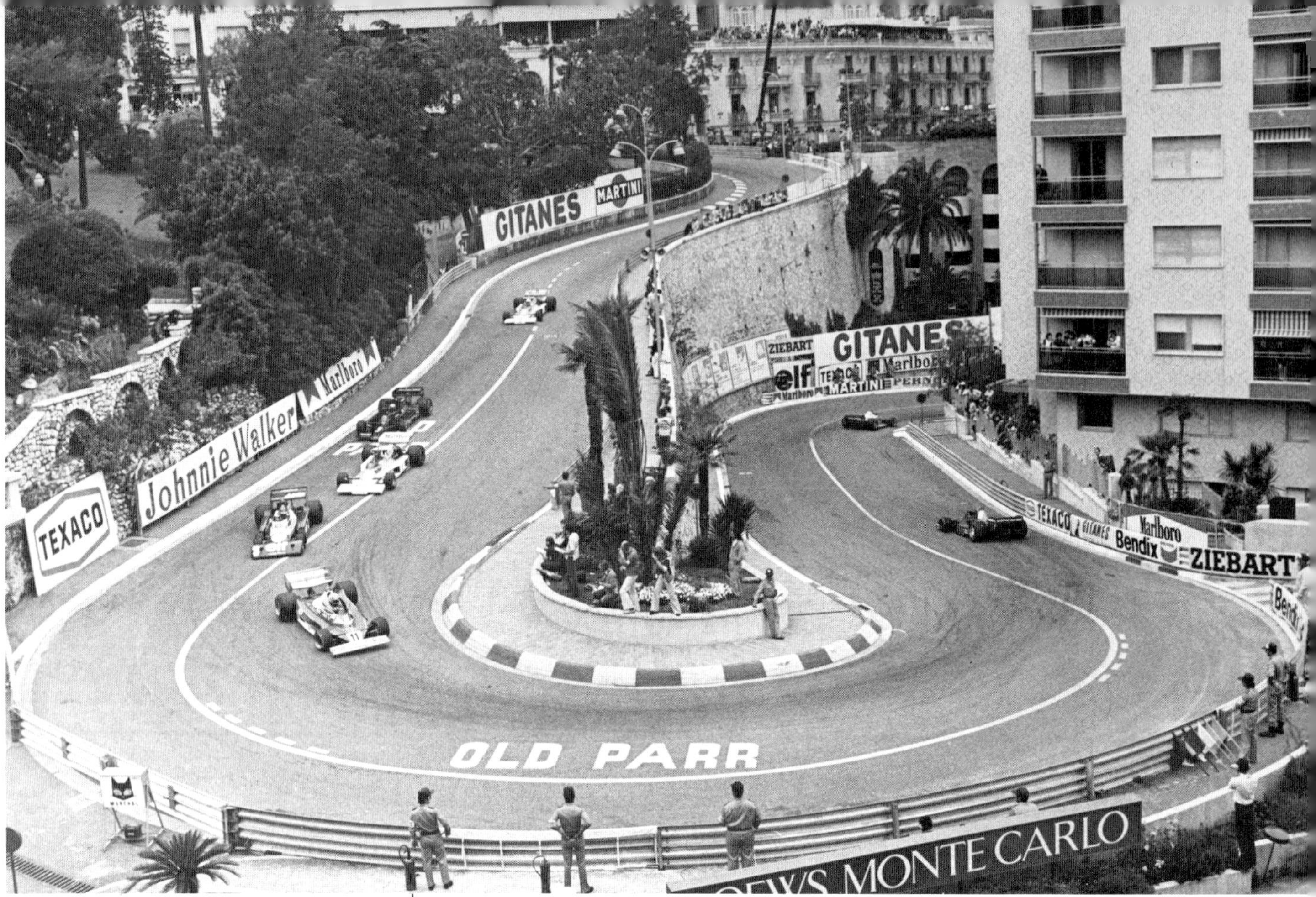

Above
The view from the Loews Hotel showing the road down from Upper Mirabeau to Lower Mirabeau.

Top right
Lauda, Hunt, Depailler and Andretti.

Right
The Ferrari team of Reutemann and Lauda.

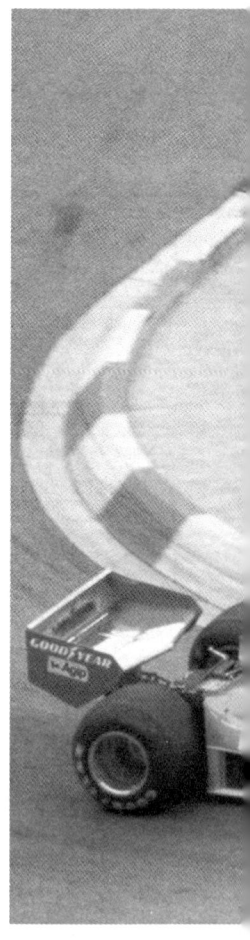

stopped and it was extinguished. The order at that stage (20 laps) was: Scheckter (Wolf), Watson (Brabham), Reutemann (Ferrari), Lauda (Ferrari), Hunt (McLaren), Andretti (Lotus), Mass (McLaren), Depailler (Tyrrell), Jones (Shadow), Brambilla (Surtees), Lafitte (Ligier), Patrese (Shadow), Ickx (Ensign), Keegan (Hesketh), Fittipaldi (Fittipaldi), and Binder (Surtees).

The leaders had settled down, as was becoming customary in motor racing, to reel off a few steady laps before someone made a major effort once their fuel load was lighter. On lap 45 Watson was missing. He had failed to negotiate the old chicane and had taken to the escape road, but he was not out of the race, and had rejoined in third place. Lauda in the meantime had passed Reutemann and was now second.

Watson continued to have trouble with the chicanes, finally exiting at the Ste. Devote corner on lap 49. Scheckter's Wolf appeared to have the legs on Lauda's Ferrari and the Austrian was never able to apply the same pressure as had Watson in the first half of the race. Scheckter was able to keep his revs down and save his car in the closing stages, knowing that he had plenty in hand should Lauda get too close. He in fact allowed the Ferrari to get within three seconds much to the excitement of the partisan crowd, but they were to be disappointed. Both Ferraris were well there at the finish, showing once again how much the 312 suited the tight Monaco streets.

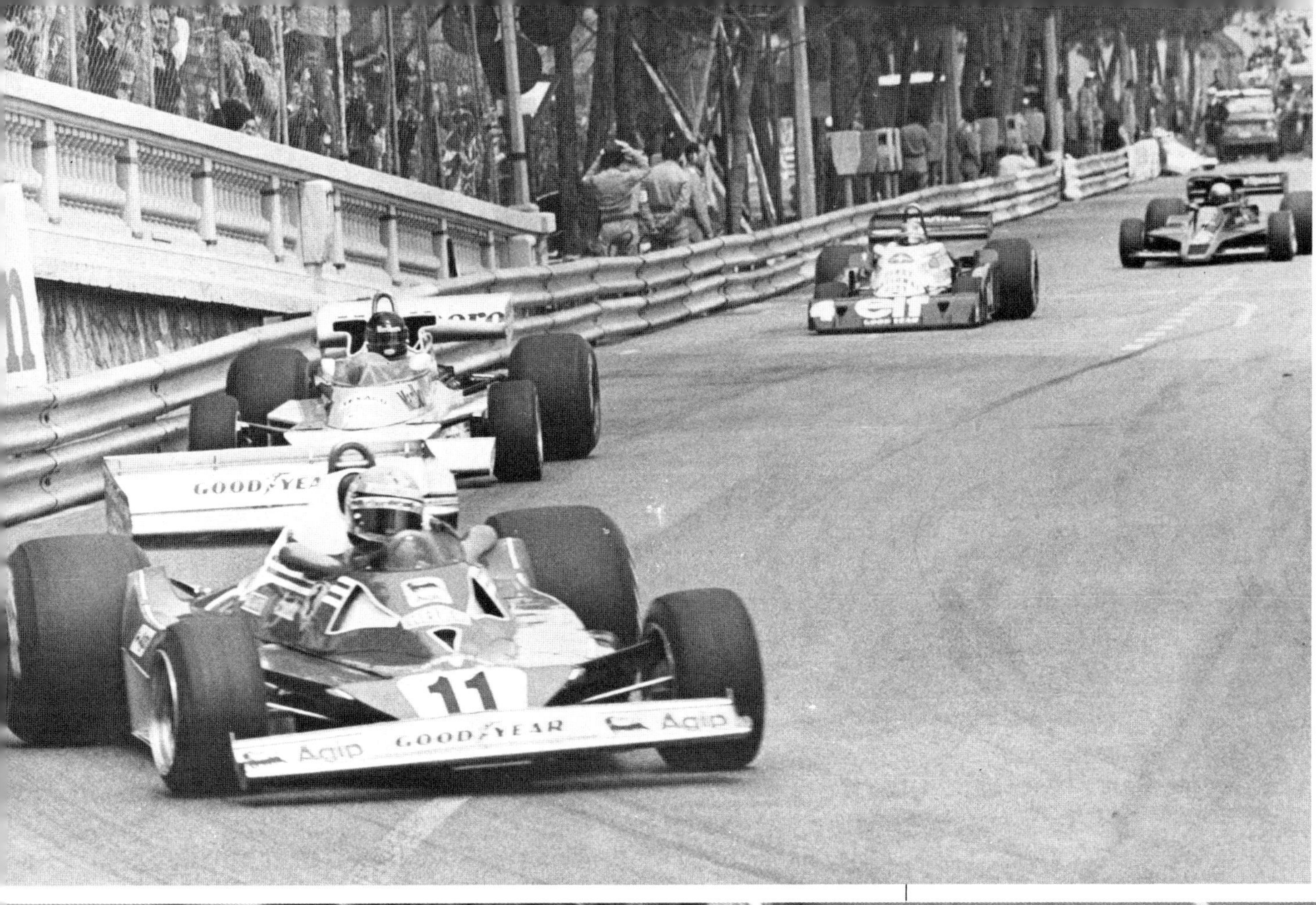
GOODYEAR
11
GOODYEAR
Agip
Agip
elf

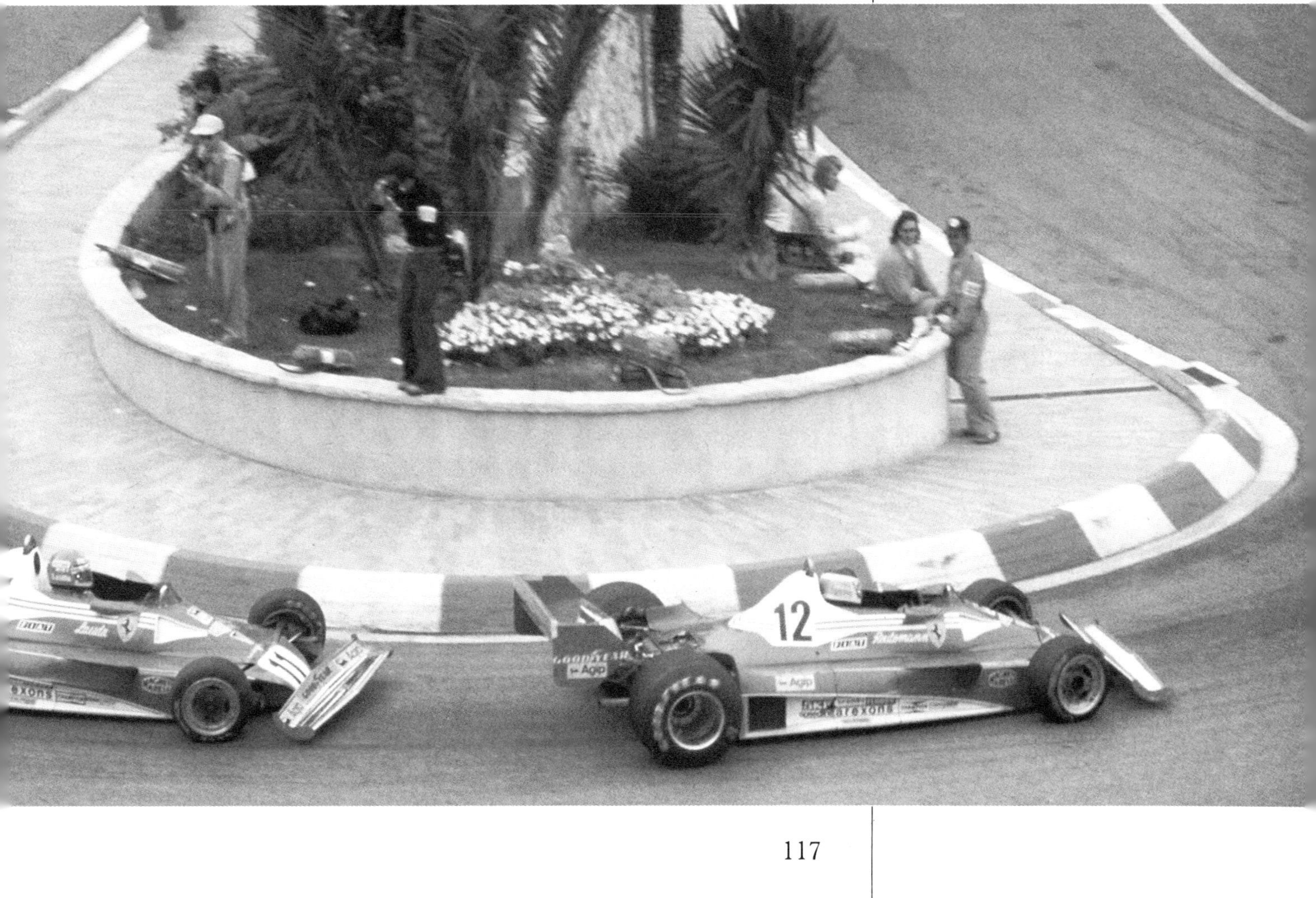
12
GOODYEAR
Agip
Agip

A regimental Jody Scheckter stands for the National Anthem.

RESULTS

1st	J.Scheckter	Wolf WR	lap 76	1 hr. 57 min. 52.77
2nd	N.Lauda	Ferrari 312T2/030	lap 76	1 hr. 57 min. 53.66
3rd	C.Reutemann	Ferrari 312T2/029	lap 76	1 hr. 58 min. 25.57
4th	J.Mass	McLaren M23/12	lap 76	1 hr. 58 min. 27.37
5th	M.Andretti	Lotus 78/3	lap 76	1 hr. 58 min. 28.32
6th	A.Jones	Shadow DN8/3A	lap 76	1 hr. 58 min. 29.38
7th	J.Laffitte	Ligier JS7/02	lap 76	1 hr. 58 min. 57.21
8th	V.Brambilla	Surtees TS19/06	lap 76	1 hr. 59 min. 01.41
9th	R.Patrese	Shadow DN8/1A	lap 75	
10th	J.Ickx	Ensign MN06	lap 75	
11th	J-P.Jarier	Hesketh 308E/1	lap 74	
12th	R.Keegan	Hesketh 308E/1	lap 73	

Fastest Lap: J.Scheckter (Wolf WR1) 1 min. 31.07 130.923 k.p.h.

Retired: R.Peterson *(Tyrrell P34/5),* lap 10, brakes; H.J.Stuck *(Brabham BT45/1B),* lap 20, electrics; J.Hunt *(McLaren M23/8),* lap 26, engine failure, E.Fittipaldi *(Fittipaldi FD04/3)* lap 37, engine failure; H.Binder *(Surtees TS19/01)* lap 42, fuel pipe split; P.Depailler *(Tyrrell P34/7)* lap 47, gearbox failure; J.Watson *(Brabham BT45/5B)* lap 49, gearbox failure and brake trouble; G.Nilsson *(Lotus 78/2)* lap 50, gearbox; C.Pace *(Surtees TS16/02),* lap 1, accident; A.Merzario, *(Williams IR/04),* lap 1, accident; T.Schenken *(Trojan T103)* lap 1, accident; J-P.Beltoise *(B.R.M. P201/01)* lap 1, accident; V.Brambilla *(March 741/2-2),* lap 1, accident; H-J.Stuck *(March 741/1)* lap 3, accident; V.Schuppan *(Ensign MN02)* lap 5, accident; C.Reutemann *(Brabham BT44/3)* lap 6, accident; F.Migault *(B.R.M. P160/06),* lap 9, accident; M.Hailwood *(McLaren M23/1)* lap 12, accident; J.Hunt *(Hesketh 308/2)* lap 28, drive shaft broke, N.Lauda *(Ferrari 312B3/010)* lap 33, ignition failure; J.Ickx *(Lotus 72/R5)* lap 34, engine broke; H.Pescarolo *(B.R.M. P160/10)* lap 63, gearbox broke.

'78
RENAULT
GO
TURBO

The Monaco Grand Prix continued to grow in popularity as did the Formula One industry. For the 36th anniversary of the race there were originally 31 entries, and since only 24 cars were allowed to practice at any one time, two preliminary sessions had to be organised to thin down the excess. After a

ENTRIES

DRIVER	TEAM	CAR
N. Lauda	Brabham	Brabham-Alfa Romeo
J. Watson	Brabham	Brabham-Alfa Romeo
D. Pironi	Tyrrell	Tyrrell-Cosworth V8
P. Depailler	Tyrrell	Tyrrell-Cosworth V8
M. Andretti	Lotus	Lotus-Cosworth V8
R. Peterson	Lotus	Lotus-Cosworth V8
J. Hunt	McLaren	McLaren-Cosworth V8
P. Tambay	McLaren	McLaren-Cosworth V8
J. Mass	A.T.S.	March-Cosworth V8
J. P. Jarier	A.T.S.	March-Cosworth V8
C. Reutemann	Ferrari	Ferrari-Flat 12
G. Villeneuve	Ferrari	Ferrari-Flat 12
E. Fittipaldi	Fittipaldi	Fittipaldi-Cosworth V8
J. P. Jabouille	Renault	Renault-Renault V6
H. J. Stuck	A.V.S.-Shadow	Shadow-Cosworth V8
G. Regazzoni	A.V.S.-Shadow	Shadow-Cosworth V8
R. Keegan	Surtees	Surtees-Cosworth V8
V. Brambilla	Surtees	Surtees-Cosworth V8
J. Scheckter	Wolf	W.R.5-Cosworth V8
J. Ickx	Ensign	Ensign-Cosworth V8
D. Daly	Hesketh	Hesketh-Cosworth V8
H. Rebaque	Rebaque	Lotus-Cosworth V8
J. Laffite	Ligier	Ligier-Matra V12
A. Jones	Williams	Williams-Cosworth V8
B. Lunger	B & S Fabs.	McLaren-Cosworth V8
R. Arnoux	Martini	Martini-Cosworth V8
K. Rosberg	Theodore	Theodore-Cosworth V8
R. Patrese	Arrows	Arrows-Cosworth V8
R. Stommelen	Arrows	Arrows-Cosworth V8
A. Merzario	Merzario	Merzario-Cosworth V8
D. Ongais	Interscope	Shadow-Cosworth V8

STARTING GRID

	11 **C. Reutemann** 1 min. 28.34
2 **J. Watson** 1 min. 28.83	
	1 **N. Lauda** 1 min. 28.84
5 **M. Andretti** 1 min. 29.10	
	4 **P. Depailler** 1 min. 29.14
7 **J. Hunt** 1 min. 29.22	
	6 **R. Peterson** 1 min. 29.23
12 **G. Villeneuve** 1 min. 29.40	
	20 **J. Scheckter** 1 min. 29.50
27 **A. Jones** 1 min. 29.51	
	8 **P. Tambay** 1 min. 30.08
15 **J.P. Jabouille** 1 min. 30.18	
	3 **D. Pironi** 1 min. 30.55
35 **R. Patrese** 1 min. 30.59	
	26 **J. Laffite** 1 min. 30.60
22 **J. Ickx** 1 min. 30.72	
	16 **H.J. Stuck** 1 min. 31.30
18 **R. Keegan** 1 min. 31.31	
	36 **R. Stommelen** 1 min. 31.31
14 **E. Fittipaldi** 1 min. 31.36	

complex selection system had been operated there were eight cars racing for two places in the practice proper. These were Daly, Rebaque, Patrese, Stommelen, Rosberg, Lunger, Arnoux and Merzario. The Arrows team of Patrese and Stommelen were able to comfortably outclass the rest, without taking too much out of their cars before the serious business began. It is interesting in reviewing the history of a motor race to see the débuts of drivers who later became household names. In 1978 we note the first mention of Rosburg and Arnoux in far from heroic circumstances.

The "official" practice was once again divided up into three sessions - Thursday (2) and Saturday. A notable first time appearance at Monaco was the Team Renault RS01 driven by Jabouille. The two Arrows drivers now found themselves in a much tougher school and with the increased traffic were having problems in even matching their earlier times. In their efforts Patrese pushed in the front end of his first choice car and Stommelen damaged himself. Star of the Thursday practice was Reutemann in a Ferrari with the best time in both sessions. Another newcomer was Villeneuve in the second Ferrari, clearly enjoying the use of a great Monaco car. As always, Lauda and Peterson were to the fore. Scheckter in the Wolf was trying for a second consecutive win, but was hindered by recurring gear box problems. Watson ended the final session of practice by putting in a last gasp effort and displacing a complacent Lauda from the front row.

The race had once again been reduced in distance, this time to 75 laps (248.4 kilometres). The previous year's farcical rule banning overtaking at the start, had been scrubbed, which was just as well since Reutemann was very slow away from pole position causing considerable confusion on the way to Ste. Devote. Hunt had a minor collision which was to send him straight back into the pits for repairs and an unhappy Reutemann also returned to the pits. Watson led the field with Depailler and Lauda in close company. Andretti, Scheckter, Jones, Peterson, Villeneuve and the rest followed on.

Depailler settled down to put Watson under the sort of pressure that the Irishman had applied to Scheckter the previous year. Lauda sat back in third place giving the tussle time to sort itself out, and ready to pounce if the opportunity arose.

As the race approached half distance the three leaders were still nose to tail and driving perfectly. They were lapping the tail enders and their timing had to be

120

perfection to avoid losing touch with each other. Eventually, for the second year in a row, Watson lost grip in braking for the old chicane and had to take to the escape road. Depailler and Lauda led with Watson now in third place.

Just after half way Lauda lost his place when he punctured a rear tyre. The positions were then: Depailler, Watson, Scheckter, Peterson, Villeneuve, Lauda, Pironi, Patrese, Tambay. Lauda had not given up, however, and driving at ten/tenths pushed the inexperienced Villeneuve so hard that on lap 63 he lost control in the tunnel and damaged his car against the guard rails. Watson, again reliving history, lost control at the Ste. Devote chicane and dropped a place to Scheckter. Lauda was now on Watson's tail and with five laps to go passed him to take third place.

Second place came to the Austrian by default when Scheckter encountered gearbox trouble and slowed. The leader Depailler (driving a four wheel car this time) was safe however, too far away to be caught in the last few laps. This was not only Depailler's first win at Monaco, but his first ever Grand Prix victory and he and his team justifiably celebrated. Niki Lauda had set a new lap record for the circuit of 1 min. 28.65 in his chase after the leaders.

A return to four wheels gave Tyrrell a 1978 win.

THIRTY-SIXTH

GRAND PRIX
OF MONACO

RESULTS

1st	P.Depailler	Tyrrell 008/3	lap 75	1 hr. 55 min. 14.66
2nd	N.Lauda	Brabham BT46/4	lap 75	1 hr. 55 min. 37.11
3rd	J.Scheckter	(Wolf WR1)	lap 75	1 hr. 55 min. 46.95
4th	J.Watson	Brabham BT46/3	lap 75	1 hr. 55 min. 48.19
5th	D.Pironi	Tyrrell 008/4	lap 75	1 hr. 56 min. 22.72
6th	R.Patrese	Arrows FA1/2	lap 75	1 hr. 56 min. 23.43
7th	P.Tambay	McLaren M26/5	lap 74	
8th	C.Reutemann	Ferrari 312T3/032	lap 74	
9th	E.Fittipaldi	Fittipaldi F5/2A	lap 74	
10th	J-P.Jabouille	Renault RS01/02	lap 71	
11th	M.Andretti	Lotus 78/3	lap 69	

Fastest lap: N.Lauda (Brabham BT46/4), lap 72, 1 min. 28.65 134.649 k.p.h.

Retired: R.Keegan *(Surtees TS19/02)*, lap 9, transmission failure; J.Laffitte *(Ligier JS9/01)* lap 12, gearbox failure; H.J.Stuck *(Shadow DN9/1A)* lap 24, accident damage to steering; J.Ickx *(Ensign MN06)* lap 27, brake trouble; A.Jones *(Williams FW06/001)*, lap 30, loss of oil; R.Stommelen *(Arrows FA1/1)*, lap 36, driver fatigue; J.Hunt *(McLaren M26/4)* lap 43, broken rear roll bar; R.Peterson *(Lotus 78/2)* lap 56, broken gearbox; G.Villeneuve *(Ferrari 312T/134)* lap 63, accident

Monaco celebrated fifty years of motor racing on the city circuit. In this time 36 Grand Prix had been run, the war plus a few missed years accounting for the difference. The cars over that period had naturally developed beyond all recognition, but the engineers and designers had not changed. They were dedicated professionals in 1929 and they were the same in 1979. The drivers were quite different. Gone was the day of the rich amateur. The driver of the day was as dedicated and professional as his back up team of engineers. Motor racing had always been a sport for the rich, now it was also a rich sport. Commercial exploitation was the reason.

ENTRIES

DRIVER	TEAM	CAR
M. Andretti	Lotus	Lotus-Cosworth V8
C. Reutemann	Lotus	Lotus-Cosworth V8
D. Pironi	Tyrrell	Tyrrell-Cosworth V8
J. P. Jarier	Tyrrell	Tyrrell-Cosworth V8
N. Lauda	Brabham	Brabham-Alfa Romeo
N. Piquet	Brabham	Brabham-Alfa Romeo
J. Watson	McLaren	McLaren-Cosworth V8
P. Tambay	McLaren	McLaren-Cosworth V8
H. J. Stuck	A.T.S.	A.T.S.-Cosworth V8
J. Scheckter	Ferrari	Ferrari Flat 12
G. Villeneuve	Ferrari	Ferrari Flat 12
E. Fittipaldi	Fittapaldi	Fittipaldi-Cosworth V8
J-P. Jabouille	Renault	Renault V6
R. Arnoux	Renault	Renault V6
J. Lammers	Shadow	Shadow-Cosworth V8
E. de Angelis	Shadow	Shadow-Cosworth V8
J. Hunt	Wolf	Wolf-Cosworth V8
D. Daly	Ensign	Ensign-Cosworth V8
G. Brancatelli	Merzario	Merzario-Cosworth V8
P. Depailler	Ligier	Ligier-Cosworth V8
J. Laffite	Ligier	Ligier-Cosworth V8
A. Jones	Williams	Williams-Cosworth V8
G. Reggazoni	Williams	Williams-Cosworth V8
R. Patrese	Arrows	Arrows-Cosworth V8
J. Mass	Arrows	Arrows-Cosworth V8

STARTING GRID

	11
	J. Scheckter
12	1 min. 26.45
G. Villeneuve	
1 min. 26.52	25
	P. Depailler
5	1 min. 27.11
N. Lauda	
1 min. 27.21	26
	J. Laffite
4	1 min. 27.26
J. P. Jarier	
1 min. 27.42	3
	D. Pironi
30	1 min. 27.42
J. Mass	
1 min. 27.47	27
	A. Jones
20	1 min. 27.67
J. Hunt	
1 min. 27.96	2
	C. Reutemann
9	1 min. 27.99
H. J. Stuck	
1 min. 28.22	1
	M. Andretti
7	1 min. 28.23
J. Watson	
1 min. 28.23	29
	R. Patrese
28	1 min. 28.30
G. Regazzoni	
1 min. 28.48	14
	E. Fittipaldi
5	1 min. 28.49
N. Piquet	
1 min. 28.52	16
	R. Arnoux
15	1 min. 28.57
J. P. Jabouille	
1 min. 28.68	

Motor racing is a spectacular sport with exciting vehicles which are ideal for carrying advertising. The commercial interests realised the potential in the '60s and pumped large amounts of money into sponsorship of the racing teams. A Lotus racing car was no longer called a Type 78 - it was a John Player Special. A McLaren M26 was now a Marlboro McLaren.

The circuit of Monaco was the advertising man's dream. Spectacular surroundings, glamorous people, high media exposure. No matter that the circuit was not ideal for the modern Grand Prix car - commercial interests prevailed and the future of the race was secure.

The 1979 race attracted another large entry of 25 and since only 24 cars were allowed into the official practice sessions, a preliminary elimination run was required. Stuck, Mass and Brancetelli were sent off for a one hour run which resulted in Brancatelli's disappointment.

The official timed runs were in two sessions, on the Thursday and Saturday, preceded by one hour untimed testing sessions. Once again the Ferrari team dominated the rest with Villeneuve and Scheckter both breaking the 1 min. 27 barrier. The Renault turbocharged car, with its massive state sponsorship was still attracting a great deal of attention, but the results were unexciting, proving that you cannot simply buy success. It is important to note the introduction of this line of development, however, because it was the forerunner of what eventually became a change of engineering policy by the whole grand prix circus.

Race day this time was dry, but dull and grey. Scheckter made the most of his pole position, but his team mate and Depailler were overtaken by Lauda in the Brabham. The leader with his adrenalin in full flow and a clear circuit ahead, was throwing the Ferrari all over the road in the most exhuberant manner. Lauda in contrast was as smooth and tidy as ever and though a gap had opened up, it was surely unlikely that Scheckter could last the whole race driving in that manner.

Villeneuve had no intention of sitting behind Lauda for too long and in a desperate effort elbowed his way past before the chicane at Ste. Devote. Ferrari first and second! Behind Lauda were Depailler (Ligier), Lafitte (Ligier), Pironi (Tyrrell), Jones (Williams), Mass (Arrows), Jarier (Tyrrell), Reutemann (Lotus), Andretti (Lotus), and Hunt (Wolf). These being the only ones in any sort of contention even after just three laps.

Unperturbed by Villeneuve, Lauda continued to

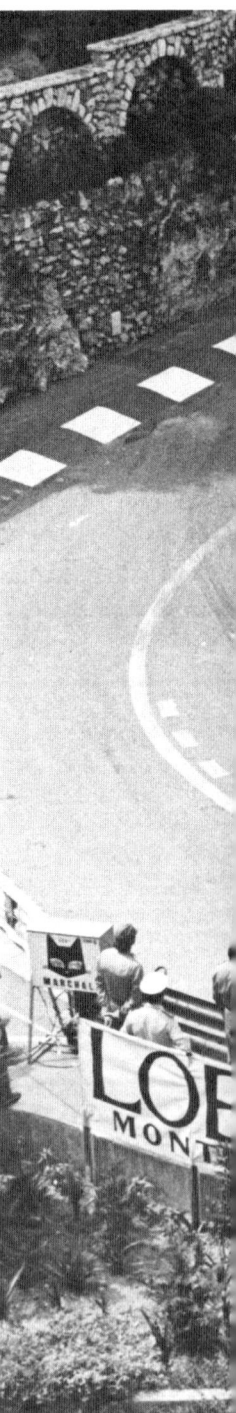

drive Monaco as he always drove Monaco - quickly but smoothly. Scheckter and Villeneuve in contrast had every intention of getting to the finish as soon as possible - if their cars held together. A number of the drivers behind Lauda were of the same temperament and Lauda was definitely holding them up.

Left
The Lotus 79 with Reutemann at the wheel flat out emerging from the tunnel.

The first lap procession seen from the Loews Hotel.

Above
Clay Regazzoni in the Frank Williams FW07.

Right
Reutemann and the Lotus in Casino Square.

After 13 laps the two Ferraris were driving a team race and their pits informed them of their comfortable lead. Depailler could not get by Lauda in order to put in a challenge and Lafitte had to stop for a new wheel. Pironi in fifth place became impatient with Depailler and after a minor 'coming together' caused him to spin. He then set about Lauda in the same reckless way. As they drove down the hill from the Casino their wheels came into contact and the Tyrrell launched itself into the air before wrecking itself on the barriers. Lauda's Brabham was also badly damaged and retired. Neither driver was hurt, but Pironi was not the most popular driver around for a time!

The Ferrai 312 was well suited to the tight Monaco circuit and generally did well.

On the same lap Andretti had retired with a suspension breakage, so the order was: Scheckter, Villeneuve, Jones, Mass, Jarier, Reutemann. Jones in the Williams was now the combination to watch. It took the Australian a number of laps to close the gap on the Ferraris, but they were still running in team formation. There was little chance that Jones would get by when the Ferraris had so much power in hand.

On lap 43 Jones damaged a wheel in a scrape along the Armco and his race was over. The two leaders were well clear of Regazzoni and just had to keep going to win. But on lap 54 the transmission broke on the Villeneuve car and the Ferrari team crossed their fingers (or whatever the Italians cross), and hoped for the best. Regazzoni in the second Williams car, saw a glimmer of a chance and put all he and his car had into closing the gap on the leader.

In spite of a magnificent effort the lead was just too much and though Regazzoni closed to within a second, Scheckter ran out the winner, having led from start to finish.

THIRTY-SEVENTH
GRAND PRIX
OF MONACO
RESULTS

1st	J.Scheckter	Ferrari 312 T4/040	lap 76	1 hr. 55 min. 22.48
2nd	G.Regazzoni	Williams FW07/002	lap 76	1 hr. 55 min. 22.92
3rd	C.Reutemann	Lotus 79/4	lap 76	1 hr. 55 min. 31.05
4th	J.Watson	McLaren M28/3C	lap 76	1 hr. 56 min. 03.79
5th	P.Depailler	Ligier JS11/03	lap 75	
6th	J.Mass	Arrows A1/05	lap 69	
7th	N.Piquet	Brabham BT48/03	lap 68	
8th	J-P.Jabouille	Renault RS10/024	lap 68	

Fastest lap: P.Depaillier (Ligier JS11/03), lap 69, 1 min. 28.82 134.240 k.p.h.

Retired: R.Patrese *(Arrows A1/06)*, lap 4, bent front suspension; J.Hunt *(Wolf WR7)* lap 5, broken drive-shaft; R.Arnoux *(Renault RS10/01)* lap 8, deranged steering; E.Fittipaldi *(Fittipaldi F5A/1)* lap 17, engine failure; M.Andretti *(Lotus 80/1)* lap 22, rear suspension failure; D.Pironi *(Tyrrell 009/4)* lap 22, accident; N.Lauda *(Brabham BT48/04)* lap 22, accident; H.J.Stuck *(ATS D2/03)* lap 31, lost wheel; J-P.Jarier *(Tyrrell 009/3)* lap 34, suspension failure; A.Jones *(Williams FW07/003)* lap 43, bent steering arm; G.Villeneuve *(Ferrari 312 T4/039)* lap 54, broken transmission; J.Laffite *(Ligier JS11/02)* lap 56, broken gearbox; N.Piquet *(Brabham BT48/03)* lap 69, broken drive-shaft; P.Depailler *(Ligier JS11/03)* lap 75, engine failure

The 1980 winner Carlos Reutemann
with his Williams Cosworth V8.

LIGIER
AND
WILLIAMS

As we come to the first race of the '80s it is probably worthwhile to review the development trends of the Formula One 3-litre cars since their introduction in 1966. The major trend had been governed by the success of the Ford-Cosworth V8 engine which had enabled many small teams to build a good car to almost a standard format. This resulted in starting grids made up from many very similar cars and other means had to be found to gain an edge. The 'handling' of the car became the key development area.

Aerodynamics were closely studied and wings sprouted at the front and rear of the cars. The major teams spent a good deal of time and money experimenting in wind tunnel facilities in order to achieve improved

ENTRIES

DRIVER	TEAM	CAR
J. Scheckter	Ferrari	Ferrari 312T5-Flat 12
G. Villeneuve	Ferrari	Ferrari-312T5-Flat 12
J-P. Jarier	Tyrrell	Tyrrell-Cosworth V8
D. Daly	Tyrrell	Tyrrell-Cosworth V8
N. Piquet	Brabham	Brabham-Cosworth V8
R. Zunino	Brabham	Brabham-Cosworth V8
J. Watson	McLaren	McLaren-Cosworth V8
A. Prost	McLaren	McLaren-Cosworth V8
J. Lammers	A.T.S.	A.T.S. D4-Cosworth V8
E. de Angelis	Lotus	Lotus 81-Cosworth V8
T. Needell	Ensign	Ensign MN14
J-P. Jabouille	Renault	Renault V6
G. Lees	Shadow	Shadow-Cosworth V8
D. Kennedy	Shadow	Shadow-Cosworth V8
E. Fittipaldi	Fittipaldi	Fittipaldi-Cosworth V8
K. Rosberg	Fittipaldi	Fittipaldi-Cosworth V8
P. Depailler	Alfa Romeo	Alfa Romeo-V12
G. Giacomelli	Alfa Romeo	Alfa Romeo-V12
D. Pironi	Ligier	Ligier-Cosworth V8
J. Laffite	Ligier	Ligier-Cosworth V8
A. Jones	Williams	Williams-Cosworth V8
C. Reutemann	Williams	Williams-Cosworth V8
R. Patrese	Arrows	Arrows-Cosworth V8
J. Mass	Arrows	Arrows-Cosworth V8
E. Cheever	Arrows	Osella-Cosworth V8

129

STARTING GRID

25
D. Pironi
1 min. 24.81

28
C. Reutemann
1 min. 24.88

27
A. Jones
1 min. 25.20

5
N. Piquet
1 min. 25.36

26
J. Laffite
1 min. 25.51

2
G. Villeneuve
1 min. 26.10

22
P. Depailler
1 min. 26.21

23
B. Giacomelli
1 min. 26.23

3
J.-P. Jarier
1 min. 26.37

8
A. Prost
1 min. 26.83

29
R. Patrese
1 min. 26.83

4
D. Daly
1 min. 26.84

9
J. Lammers
1 min. 26.88

12
E. de Angelis
1 min. 26.93

30
J. Mass
1 min. 26.96

15
J-P. Jabouille
1 min. 27.10

1
J. Scheckter
1 min. 27.18

20
E. Fittipaldi
1 min. 27.49

down force and therefore better grip on the road. Of course, the basis of grip has to be the tyres. Dunlop had been the foremost developer of the racing tyre in the early post war years, but when they withdrew to concentrate on normal road going tyres, the mantle was taken up by the major companies of Goodyear, Michelin and Firestone. Tyre chemistry had developed specialised compounds to suit each surface condition. There were even qualifying compounds which were only good for about three fast laps.

1979/80 saw the introduction of the so called 'skirt'. The extension of the bodywork almost to the ground helped to reduce the amount of air below the car therefore almost creating a vacuum which sucked the car onto the road.

At the end of the '70s the Cosworth engine was reaching the end of its development, putting out nearly 500 b.h.p. The aerodynamic and ground effects developments had been taken pretty well as far as they could go. The pointer for the future was introduced by Renault with the twin-turbo charged 1½-litre engine, at this time yet to achieve much success, but attracting the interest of everyone.

Previous races at Monaco had limited practice to 24 cars but for 1980 25 cars were allowed for qualification. This was not popular with the major teams since it meant overcrowding but the organisers had their way, maintaining their reputation for inconsistency.

Favourites in practice were the Ligier team of Pironi and Lafitte. The team had invested a great deal of time in preparation for this race and their cars were well set up. The best times in the previous year's qualifying had just squeezed below 1 min. 27. The same time would gain only the tenth place on the 1980 grid. The Williams team of Jones and Reutemann were also maintaining their steady progress, sharing the leading positions. The new Ferraris were disappointing after performances in recent Monaco races made them almost automatic favourites.

For the second year in a row the race was to be held over 76 laps of the circuit. Pironi led the way, followed by Jones, Reutemann, Lafitte and Depailler. As the rest crowded into the bottleneck at Ste. Devote, Daly touched wheels with Giacomelli and was launched into space, finally landing on the top of the Tyrrell of Jarier. Prost ran into the wreckage and four cars were out almost before the race had started.

The Ligier/Williams battle was expected and Pironi

Left
**The Brabham BT49 showing its very
clean front profile ...**

... compared with the Ferrari. *Above*

and Jones set to it at the front, with Reutemann and
Lafitte in close attendance. This situation continued for
25 laps until Jones suddenly went missing with a broken
gearbox. Reutemann in the second Williams immediately took his place and continued to keep the pressure on
the leader.

At the half way stage the order was: Pironi (Ligier),
Reutemann (Williams), Lafitte (Ligier), Depailler (Alfa

131

Lafitte inherited a fortunate second place when cars ahead failed late in the race.

Romeo), Piquet (Brabham), de Angelis (Lotus), Mass (Arrows) and the rest. Reutemann settled down to lap steadily, not risking any overtaking with the erratic Pironi at this stage. His patience was rewarded on lap 55, when the Ligier jumped out of gear on the hill down to Mirabeau and he ran into the guard rail. The car was too damaged to continue. At the same time the second Ligier was also losing power and was no threat to the leader.

Light rain towards the end of the race made the circuit quite slippery and overtaking virtually out of the question, so Reutemann had a comfortable run to the flag.

THIRTY-EIGHTH

G R A N D   P R I X
O F   M O N A C O
R E S U L T S

1st	C.Reutemann	Williams FW078/5	lap 76	1 hr. 55 min. 34.365
2nd	J.Laffite	Ligier JS11/15/03	lap 76	1 hr. 56 min. 47.994
3rd	N.Piquet	Brabham BT49/7	lap 76	1 hr. 56 min. 52.091
4th	J.Mass	Arrows A3/4	lap 75	
5th	G.Villeneuve	Ferrari 312T5/045	lap 75	
6th	E.Fittipaldi	Fittipaldi F7/1	lap 74	
7th	M.Andretti	Lotus 81/2	lap 73	
8th	R.Patrese	Arrows A3/5	lap 73	
9th	E.de Angelis	Lotus 81/3	not running at finish	
10th	J.Lammers	ATS D4/02	lap 64	

Fastest Lap: C.Reutemann (Williams FW078/5) lap 48, 1 min. 27.418 136.393 k.p.h.

Retired: D.Daly *(Tyrrell 010/3)* lap 1, accident; B.Giacomelli *(Alfa Romeo 179/02)*, lap 1, accident; A.Prost *(McLaren M29C/4)* lap 1, accident; J-P.Jarier *(Tyrrell)* lap 1 accident; A.Jones *(Williams FW07B/7)* lap 25, broken differential. J-P.Jabouille *(Renault RE23)* lap 26, broken gearbox; J.Scheckter *(Ferrari 312 T5/046)*, lap 27, gave up; P.Depailler *(Ligier JS11/15/04)* lap 55, accident; E.de Angelis *(Lotus 81/3)* accident on lap 69

The 1981 Formula One season started with controversy. Motor racing's governing body F.I.S.A. (Federation International du Sport Automobile) brought in a ruling which attempted to ban 'skirts'. The 'skirt' was the extension of the body work which reduced the amount of air passing under the car, effectively causing a vacuum and increased down force. The new ruling allowed only a minimum of six centimetres clearance between ground and bodywork. The manufacturers immediately set about finding ways around the rule and by the time Monaco came around it was obvious that most of the major teams had driver adjustable ride height built

ENTRIES

DRIVER	TEAM	CAR
A. Jones	Williams	Williams-Cosworth V8
C. Reutemann	Williams	Williams-Cosworth V8
E. Cheever	Tyrrell	Tyrrell-Cosworth V8
M. Alboreto	Tyrrell	Tyrrell-Cosworth V8
N. Piquet	Brabham	Brabham-Cosworth V8
H. Rebaque	Brabham	Brabham-Cosworth V8
J. Watson	McLaren	McLaren-Cosworth V8
A. de Cesaris	McLaren	McLaren-Cosworth V8
E. de Angelis	Lotus	Lotus-Cosworth V8
N. Mansell	Lotus	Lotus-Cosworth V8
M. Surer	Ensign	Ensign-Cosworth V8
A. Prost	Renault	Renault V6 t/c
R. Arnoux	Renault	Renault V6 t/c
K. Rosberg	Fittipaldi	Fittipaldi-Cosworth V8
F. Serra	Fittipaldi	Fittipaldi-Cosworth V8
M. Andretti	Alfa Romeo	Alfa Romeo V12
B. Giacomelli	Alfa Romeo	Alfa Romeo V12
J.-P. Jabouille	Talbot	Talbot-Matra V12
J. Laffite	Talbot	Talbot-Matra V12
G. Villeneuve	Ferrari	Ferrari V6 t/c
D. Pironi	Ferrari	Ferrari V6 t/c
R. Patrese	Arrows	Arrows-Cosworth V8
S. Stohr	Arrows	Arrows-Cosworth V8
G. Gabbiani	Osella	Osella-Cosworth V8
P. Carlo Ghinzani	Osella	Osella-Cosworth V8
P. Tambay	Theodore	Theodore-Cosworth

133

STARTING GRID

5
N. Piquet
1 min. 25.71

27
G. Villeneuve
1 min. 25.78

12
N. Mansell
1 min. 25.81

2
C. Reutemann
1 min. 26.01

29
R. Patrese
1 min. 26.04

11
E. de Angelis
1 min. 26.26

1
A. Jones
1 min. 26.54

26
J. Laffite
1 min. 26.70

15
A. Prost
1 min. 26.95

7
J. Watson
1 min. 27.06

8
A. de Cesaris
1 min. 27.12

22
M. Andretti
1 min. 27.51

16
R. Arnoux
1 min. 27.51

30
S. Stohr
1 min. 27.56

3
E. Cheever
1 min. 27.59

33
P. Tambay
1 min. 27.94

28
D. Pironi
1 min. 28.27

23
B. Giacomelli
1 min. 28.32

14
M. Surer
1 min. 28.34

4
M. Arboreto
1 min. 28.36

Right
Villeneuve leading Patrese.

Below
Patrese in the clean lined Arrows
Cosworth. The combination retired
after 30 laps with gear box failure.

in. On the circuit their cars were well below the six centimetre limit, but as they entered the pits and passed the electronic measuring light they were once again legal! Call it bending the rules if you like, but there was little doubt that it was cheating, in the opinion of most outsiders.

There was a record entry of 32 drivers to be reduced down to the 26 allowed to practice, so a preliminary elimination got rid of some of the dead wood. After a couple of withdrawals there were in fact 25 cars on the circuit for practice.

The most notable new car was the Ferrari with 1½-litre turbocharged engine. Ignoring the Renault lack of success over the previous two seasons Enzo Ferrari had made the bold decision to drop the faithful flat 12 cylinder engine. The turbocharged engine was extremely powerful but, as was common with this type of engine, suffered from throttle lag. In effect the engine did not instantly respond to the throttle pedal, so that the drivers had to learn a whole new technique of applying throttle pressure before it was actually required.

Of the two Ferrari drivers Villeneuve adapted to the new technique very quickly but Pironi found it difficult. The number one driver achieved 1 min. 25.79 which gave him a place on the first row of the starting grid. but Pironi could only manage 1 min. 28.27 and was in amongst the also rans.

Star of the practice show was Nelson Piquet in the Brabham which was so superior to almost everything else that there were whispers that the car had to be underweight or over three litres - or something! Nobody had the conviction to make an official protest however. Notable for British fans was the début appearance of Nigel Mansell in a Lotus, incidentally scoring an impressive third place on the grid.

In beautiful sunny conditions the start time was delayed by a fire at a hotel within the circuit. Eventually at 4.30 p.m. the race was under way even though there were overtaking restrictions in the tunnel. Piquet was away first from pole position but the annual collision occurred at the Ste. Devote chicane. This time it was de Cesaris and Andretti who were eliminated immediately, but Prost and Surer also suffered minor damage.

Piquet very quickly opened up a gap between himself and Villeneuve. Mansell, Reutemann, Jones, Patrese, de Angelis and Lafitte were all there competing strongly. The leaders settled down to knock off a few steady laps and to reduce their fuel load before trying anything dramatic. On lap 14 Reutemann, who was tailing Mansell, got a little bit too close and nudged the Lotus. The damage to the Williams cost him a trip to the pits for new bodywork, after which he rejoined the race in 15th place. Mansell's car was more seriously damaged and the Lotus pit would not allow him to restart.

The World Champion Alan Jones accepted his gift

Above
The Talbot Matra V12 in the hands of Jacques Lafitte.

Bottom left
World Champion Alan Jones with Patrese and de Angelis at Tabac.

Top left
Villeneuve and Mansell.

Left
Villeneuve (Ferrari) leading Mansell (Lotus), Reutemann (Williams) and Jones (Williams).

of third place and promptly moved on to pass the Ferrari. Piquet was able to hold Jones at arms length until they began to lap the tail-enders. Jones was much more skilled than Piquet and in the process closed the gap to nothing. For several laps they circled like prize fighters with Villeneuve sitting in third place waiting for the show down! de Angelis and Arnoux had retired leaving Laffite fourth and Watson fifth. The leading five cars were the only ones left on the same lap at the half way stage. A stalemate existed at the front for lap after lap, but as fatigue began to set in, Piquet was the one who made the mistake, when he took the wrong line at the Tabac corner and slid into the crash barrier.

The turbo victory for Gilles Villeneuve and Ferrari.

Jones had no sooner smiled in satisfaction at being in the lead, than his Williams began to give fuel problems. As a precaution he made a lightning visit to the pits for more fuel and still held first place from Villeneuve, although the margin was much reduced. With only ten laps to go the two leaders were both far from healthy mechanically speaking. Villeneuve decided to gamble for a win and increased his pace, knowing full well that the new Ferrari might not last the effort. The gamble was to pay off and he took the lead on lap 72, much to Jones frustration, but there was little that he could do with the Williams misfiring badly.

The new 1½-litre turbocharged Ferrari had won its first race and the pattern was taking shape for the future. The other teams took note!

THIRTY-NINETH
GRAND PRIX
OF MONACO
RESULTS

1st	G.Villeneuve	Ferrari 126CK/052	lap 76	1 hr. 54 min. 23.38
2nd	A.Jones	Williams FW07C/15	lap 76	1 hr. 55 min. 03.29
3rd	J.Laffite	Talbot JS17	lap 76	1 hr. 55 min. 52.62
4th	D.Pironi	Ferrari 126CK/050	lap 75	
5th	E.Cheever	Tyrrell 010	lap 74	
6th	M.Surer	Ensign MN15	lap 72	
7th	P.Tambay	Theodore TY/02	lap 72	

Fastest lap: A.Jones (Williams FW07C), lap 48, 1 min. 27.47 136.311 k.p.h.

Retired: M.Andretti *(Alfa Romeo V12)*, lap 1, accident; A.de Cesaris *(McLaren MP4/1)* lap 1, accident; S.Stohr *(Arrows A3)* lap 15, electrical trouble; N.Mansell *(Lotus 87.1)* lap 16, rear suspension broken; R.Patrese *(Arrows A3)* lap 30, gearbox failure; R.Arnoux *(Renault RE26B)* lap 33, accident; E.de Angelis *(Lotus 87/2)* lap 33, engine failure; C.Reutemann *(Williams FW07C/12)* lap 35, broken gearbox; A.Prost *(Renault RE32)* lap 46, engine failure; B.Giacomelli *(Alfa Romeo V12)*, lap 51, accident; M.Alboreto *(Tyrrell 010)* lap 51, accident; J.Watson *(McLaren MP4/2)* lap 53, engine failure; N.Piquet *(Brabham BT49/11)* lap 54, accident

'82
PATRESE WITH A PUSH !

The progressive change over from the old Cosworth V8 powered car to 1½-litres turbocharged continued though still in its early days. Among the entry for the 1982 Monaco Grand Prix were the Renault team which had been turbocharged for several years, and the Ferrari team, which had changed engines in the previous season. Brabham now had one car with a four-cylinder B.M.W. turbocharged engine for their number

ENTRIES

DRIVER	TEAM	CAR
N. Piquet	Brabham	Brabham-BMW t/c
R. Patrese	Brabham	Brabham-Cosworth V8
M. Alboreto	Tyrrell	Tyrrell-Cosworth V8
B. Henton	Tyrrell	Tyrrell-Cosworth V8
D. Daly	Williams	Williams-Cosworth V8
K. Rosberg	Williams	Williams-Cosworth V8
J. Watson	McLaren	McLaren-Cosworth V8
N. Lauda	McLaren	McLaren-Cosworth V8
M. Winkelhock	A.T.S.	A.T.S.-Cosworth V8
E. Salazar	A.T.S.	A.T.S.-Cosworth V8
E. de Angelis	Lotus	Lotus-Cosworth V8
N. Mansell	Lotus	Lotus-Cosworth V8
R. Guerrero	Ensign	Ensign-Cosworth V8
A. Prost	Renault	Renault V6
R. Arnoux	Renault	Renault V6
J. Mass	March	March-Cosworth V8
R. Boesel	March	March-Cosworth V8
E. de Villota	March	March-Cosworth V8
F. Serra	Fittipaldi	Fittipaldi-Cosworth V8
A. de Cesaris	Alfa Romeo	Alfa Romeo V12
B. Giacomelli	Alfa Romeo	Alfa Romeo V12
E. Cheever	Talbot	Matra V12
J. Laffite	Talbot	Matra V12
D. Pironi	Ferrari	Ferrari V6 t/c
M. Surer	Arrows	Arrows-Cosworth V8
M. Baldi	Arrows	Arrows-Cosworth V8
J.-P. Jarier	Osella	Osella-Cosworth V8
R. Paletti	Osella	Osella-Cosworth V8
J. Lammers	Theodore	Cosworth V8
D. Warwick	Toleman	Hart 415R t/c
T. Fabi	Toleman	Hart 415R t/c

139

STARTING GRID

16
A. Arnoux
1 min. 23.28

2
R. Patrese
1 min. 23.79

23
B. Giacomelli
1 min. 23.94

15
A. Prost
1 min. 24.44

28
D. Pironi
1 min. 24.59

6
K. Rosberg
1 min. 24.65

22
A. de Cesaris
1 min. 24.93

5
D. Daly
1 min. 25.39

3
M. Alboreto
1 min. 25.45

7
J. Watson
1 min. 25.58

12
N. Mansell
1 min. 25.64

8
N. Lauda
1 min. 25.84

1
N. Piquet
1 min. 26.08

9
M. Winkelhock
1 min. 26.26

11
E. de Angelis
1 min. 26.46

25
E. Cheever
1 min. 26.46

4
B. Henton
1 min. 26.69

26
J. Laffite
1 min. 27.01

29
M. Surer
1 min. 27.02

10
E. Salazar
1 min. 27.02

one driver Nelson Piquet, as well as their customary BT49-Cosworth V8 for Patrese. We also had the new Toleman team with the Toleman-Hart 415R turbocharged for drivers Warwick and Fabi. McLaren had also announced that they were building a new Porsche turbocharged engine car for the 1983 season, which was exciting news.

The Formula One world was still in an unhappy frame of mind. The Formula One Constructors Association (F.O.C.A.) was in frequent conflict with the sport's governing body - Federation International du Sport Automobile (F.I.S.A.). Also the Formula One drivers, who had had much to say for a number of years over safety, were constantly in conflict over the limitation of the qualifying field to 26 cars. In fact the previous year's Belgian Grand Prix had been delayed due to a drivers' strike. Even the mechanics had withdrawn their labour at the same race, because of their conditions of work!

There were frequent inter-team accusations of cheating and yet many of the F.O.C.A. teams had openly flouted the spirit of the rules over 'skirt' height. At the previous Monaco race the Brabham team had been unofficially accused of running an under-weight car. The same thing happened again during pre-qualifying for the '82 race when Mass qualified the March car and then switched to a second car, which was the one weighed by the scrutineers. The first car had been dismantled and was therefore unavailable for weighing.

Nevertheless 31 cars entered for the '82 race at Monaco which remained a very popular race both with the public and the sponsors. Again a pre-qualifying session was necessary to reduce the official session to 26 cars. The teams forced to pre-qualify were those without points in the previous season's Manufacturers Championship and they were: Mass, Boesel and Villota (March), Warwick and Fabi (Toleman), Jarier and Paletti (Osella), and Serra (Fittipaldi). The drivers felt that pre-qualifying should be judged on driver ability, but the F.O.C.A. opinion carried more weight. Three drivers were allowed through to official practice and these were Mass, Warwick and Jarier.

Official practice was held over two sessions on Thursday and Friday afternoons, preceded by untimed testing sessions. It must be remembered that the racing teams have no time to set their cars up for Monaco, other than in the pre-race qualifying unlike most other circuits, where testing can be arranged well in advance of the race. Prominent were the Renault team who were

achieving progress after several years struggling to get their cars right. Arnoux was the fastest on both Thursday and Friday with Prost close behind. Piquet in the new turbocharged Brabham qualified comfortably but his team mate, Patrese was very quick in the Cosworth powered car and gained the front row of the grid -alongside Arnoux.

141

Pironi in the sole Ferrari performed well in spite of the recent death of his friend Villeneuve. The decision to race had been left to the driver and he had bravely decided to continue. The new Toleman team were very disappointing. Fabi failed to survive the pre-qualifying and Warwick never looked like making the grid.

The start had been marred for the previous two years by crashes at the Ste. Devote chicane, which was a single file bottleneck. This time everyone got through without mishap and Arnoux in the Renault led. Giacomelli, Prost, Patrese, Pironi, de Cesaris, Alboreto and Rosberg followed. Arnoux, with the advantage of a clear circuit ahead of him, quickly opened up a considerable gap over the second car. On lap three Prost in the second Renault squeezed past Giacomelli and the French crowd were on their feet cheering them both on!

Giacomelli's first race at Monaco was not to last long because he was forced to retire with differential trouble after only five laps. The Renaults were also unable to maintain their domination for long. On lap 15 Arnoux lost grip at the swimming pool and spun in the middle of the road. His engine stalled and he was unable to restart -so, with an otherwise completely sound car he was forced to retire. His partner took up the lead and in his calm manner steadily clicked away the laps, the Renault definitely having the legs on its opposition.

The order after 32 laps was Prost (Renault), Patrese (Brabham), Pironi (Ferrari), de Cesaris (Alfa Romeo), Rosberg (Williams), Alboreto (Tyrrell), Mansell (Lotus), Daly (Williams), Watson (McLaren), Lauda (McLaren).

On the fiftieth lap Piquet retired the new Brabham which had not been running smoothly for some time. Over the next few laps, with the leaders maintaining their formation, some light rain began to fall and, though it was not enough to wet the roads, when combined with the rubber on the road, conditions became very slippery. Rosberg was caught out at the old chicane and broke a front wheel and five laps later (lap 70), Alboreto retired with a broken suspension. With only three laps to go Prost, with the race in his grasp, made his first error when overtaking tail enders at Ste. Devote, and clouted the kerb. This must have disturbed his concentration for at the old chicane he misjudged the slippery corner and spun into the barriers completely wrecking his car.

Patrese now led from Pironi, de Cesaris, Daly, de Angelis and Mansell, but the conditions were treacherous. With only two laps to go he spun at the Mirabeau and also stalled his engine. Pironi and de

142

Patrese in the Brabham BT49D.

Cesaris were past him before he could 'bump' start his car on the down slope. Patrese had now settled for third place with no chance of catching Pironi and de Cesaris, but to his surprise the Alfa Romeo was stopped on the hill up to Ste. Devote, having run out of fuel. To his further amazement he found Pironi stopped in the tunnel, with less than half a lap to go. He too had run out of fuel! So Patrese took the Renault across the line to record its first win at Monaco.

The post race inquest raised the question - 'had Patrese been push started at Mirabeau?' The Marshalls had pushed the car away from its original point of rest, for safety. But Patrese had restarted by running down the hill. If he had been disqualified there would not have been a winner since no other car completed the full distance! Fortunately there was no official protest so the result stood.

FORTIETH
GRAND PRIX
OF MONACO
RESULTS

1st	R.Patrese	Brabham BT49D/17	lap 76	1 hr. 54 min. 11.26
2nd	D.Pironi	Ferrari 126C2/059	lap 75	not running
3rd	A.de Cesaris	Alfa Romeo 182	lap 75	not running
4th	N.Mansell	Lotus 91/7	lap 75	
5th	E.de Angelis	Lotus 91/6	lap 75	
6th	D.Daly	Williams FW08/4	lap 74	not running
7th	A.Prost	Renault RE34B	lap 73	not running
8th	B.Henton	Tyrrell 011	lap 72	
9th	M.Surer	Arrows A4	lap 70	

Fastest lap: R.Patrese (Brabham BT49D/17) lap 69, 1 min. 26.354 138.073 k.p.h.

Retired: M.Alboreto *(Tyrrell 011)*, lap 70, broken suspension; K.Rosberg *(Williams FW08/3)* lap 65, accident damage; N.Lauda *(McLaren MP4/6)* lap 57, engine trouble; N.Piquet *(Brabham BT50/3)* lap 50, engine and gearbox; J.Watson *(McLaren MP4/2)* lap 36, ignition trouble; M.Winkelhock *(ATS D6)* lap 32, transmission; J.Laffite *(Talbot JS19/2)* lap 30, driver gave up; E.Cheever *(Talbot JS19/1)* lap 28, engine failure; E.Salazar *(ATS D6)* lap 23, fire extinguisher; R.Arnoux *(Renault RE37B)*, lap 15, spun and stalled; B.Giacommelli *(Alfa Romeo 182)* lap 5, driveshaft trouble

Monaco is famous for its gambling and the 1983 Monaco Grand Prix became not just a test of driver and car against one of the most difficult circuits in the world, but a gamble on the correct choice of tyres. Tyre technology had developed such specialised compounds to suit prevailing conditions that if those conditions changed during a race, the performance of the car was drastically changed. Wet weather tyres driven in dry conditions would overheat and eventually break up, and dry weather 'slicks', without any tread, if used in the wet would have no grip at all!

ENTRIES

DRIVER	TEAM	CAR
K. Rosberg	Williams	Williams-Cosworth V8
J. Laffite	Wiliams	Williams-Cosworth V8
M. Alboreto	Tyrrell	Tyrrell-Cosworth V8
D. Sullivan	Tyrrell	Tyrrell-Cosworth V8
N. Piquet	Brabham	Brabham BT52 t/c
R. Patrese	Brabham	Brabham BT52 t/c
J. Watson	McLaren	McLaren-Cosworth V8
N. Lauda	McLaren	McLaren-Cosworth V8
M. Winkelhock	A.T.S.	A.T.S.-Cosworth V8
E. de Angelis	Lotus	Lotus-Renault t/c
N. Mansell	Lotus	Lotus-Cosworth V8
A. Prost	Renault	Renault RE40 t/c
E. Cheever	Renault	Renault RE40 t/c
E. Salazar	R.A.M.-March	Ram-March-Cosworth
A. de Cesaris	Alfa Romeo	Alfa Romeo 183T
M. Baldi	Alfa Romeo	Alfa Romeo 183T
J.-P. Jarier	Ligier	Ligier-Cosworth V8
R. Boesel	Ligier	Ligier-Cosworth V8
P. Tambay	Ferrari	Ferrari 126C2 t/c
R. Arnoux	Ferrari	Ferrari 126C2 t/c
M. Surer	Arrows	Arrows-Cosworth V8
F. Serra	Arrows	Arrows-Cosworth V8

Therefore in changeable weather conditions each team had to gamble on how the weather would be

145

15
A. Prost
1 min. 24.84

28
R. Arnoux
1 min. 25.18

16
E. Cheever
1 min. 26.28

27
R. Tambay
1 min. 26.29

1
K. Rosberg
1 min. 26.30

5
N. Piquet
1 min. 27.27

22
A. de Cesaris
1 min. 27.68

2
J. Laffite
1 min. 27.73

25
J.-P. Jarier
1 min. 27.91

35
D. Warwick
1 min. 28.02

3
M. Alboreto
1 min. 28.25

29
M. Surer
1 min. 28.35

23
M. Baldi
1 min. 28.64

12
N. Mansell
1 min. 28.72

30
F. Serra
1 min. 28.78

9
M. Winkelhock
1 min. 28.97

26
R. Boesel
1 min. 29.22

6
R. Patrese
1 min. 29.20

11
E. de Angelis
1 min. 29.52

4
D. Sullivan
1 min. 29.53

throughout the two hour race. The 1983 race set each team this problem.

Once again the entry was over subscribed and a pre-qualifying session was required for those teams without manufacturers' points in the previous season. Three drivers were to qualify for the official practice and these were Warwick and Giacomelli for the Toleman team and Salazar in the lone RAM-March.

The 1983 cars were now subject to the non-ground effect rule which eliminated the 'skirts' of previous seasons. Therefore everyone came to Monaco without prior experience of suspension settings and required all the time available to prepare their cars. As before practice was in two timed sessions preceded by testing periods. The weather, however, intervened and virtually ruled out the second session and therefore any team without good times early on were unable to improve their position on the Saturday. The McLaren team was the most embarrassed of all the major teams. Watson had only been able to record 1 min. 30.28 and his colleague Lauda only a little better with 1 min. 29.90, which was not good enough, so they went home.

The morning of race day was very wet and though conditions improved by the afternoon the decision had become more difficult, because, although it was not raining, the circuit was quite wet in parts and there were no guarantees that it would not rain later.

The cars were on the starting grid while the drivers and team managers were still trying to make up their minds. Ferrari and Brabham gambled on wet weather tyres but with dry weather suspension settings. Rosberg in the Williams decided on 'slicks', but most teams split their chances by putting one car on wet weather tyres and the second on 'slicks'.

So the Monaco gamble started with Rosberg on a dry patch of road making a good start to drop into second place behind Prost. Cheever, from the dry side of the road also got away quickly to take third place. Mansell and Alboreto had a 'coming together' which eliminated both of them on the first lap.

Rosberg on 'slicks' clearly had the advantage over Prost on 'wets' and passed the Renault on the road up to Ste. Devote, as they started the second lap. The weather conditions were improving quickly and a drying wind was doing its job. So the cars on 'wets' started to return to the pits for tyre changes. Prost hung on until lap seven before he faced up to the inevitable and came into the pits, which dropped him back to eighth place.

Rosberg in the Williams now led from Lafitte (Williams), Surer (Arrows), Warwick (Toleman), Prost (Renault), de Angelis (Lotus), Piquet (Brabham), Cheever (Renault), and Jarier (Ligier). The two Williams cars settled down, well clear of the rest, to burn off the laps. The still dicey conditions were probably an advantage to Rosberg since he was forced to drive smoothly, rather than in his usual exuberant manner.

Spectators get a bird's eye view of Ste. Devote from nearby appartements.

Alain Prost in the Renault V6 turbo.

Rosberg making full use of the whole of the road in driving to his victory?

Surer held onto third place but Warwick and Piquet were evidently faster and trying to get by. On lap 50 the notorious Ste. Devote chicane claimed two more victims. Surer and Warwick both entered the corner nose to tail and collided resulting in both cars being wrecked on the Armco. Piquet inherited third place and three laps later Lafitte's gear box broke and Piquet was second. The Brabham driver was flying, but even so he could make no impression on Rosberg, who ran off the remaining laps to record probably his best ever win. Piquet was second but still 18 seconds behind the winner, but would the result have been different if he had chosen the right tyres at the start?

FORTY-FIRST
GRAND PRIX
OF MONACO
RESULTS

1st	K.Rosberg	Williams FW08C/07	lap 76	1 hr. 56 min. 38.121
2nd	N.Piquet	Brabham TB52/3	lap 76	1 hr. 56 min. 56.596
3rd	A.Prost	Renault RE40/03	lap 76	1 hr. 57 min. 09.487
4th	P.Tambay	Ferrari 126C2/065	lap 76	1 hr. 57 min. 42.418
5th	D.Sullivan	Tyrrell 011/5	lap 74	
6th	M.Baldi	Alfa Romeo 183T	lap 74	
7th	F.Serra	Arrows A6/3	lap 74	

Fastest Lap: N.Piquet (Brabham BT52/3) lap 69, 1 min. 27.283 136.603 k.p.h.

Retired: R.Patrese *(Brabham BT52/4)* lap 65, fuel system failure; J.Laffite *(Williams FW08C/08)* lap 54, gearbox failure; D.Warwick *(Toleman TG183B/02)* lap 50, accident; E.de Angelis *(Lotus 93T/1)* lap 50, broken drive shaft; M.Surer *(Arrows A6/2)* lap 50, accident; J-P.Jarier *(Ligier JS21/D4)* lap 33, hydraulic pump drive; E.Cheever *(Renault RE40/02)* lap 31, engine failure; A.de Cesaris *(Alfa Romeo 183T)* lap 14, gearbox failure; R.Arnoux *(Ferrari 126C2/064)* lap 7, accident damage; R.Boesel *(Ligier JS21/03)* lap 4, accident; M.Winkelhock *(ATS D6-02)* lap 4, accident; M.Alboreto *(Tyrrell 011/4)* lap 1, accident; N.Mansell *(Lotus 92/10)* lap 1, accident

When the 27 entries arrived for the 42nd running of the Monaco Grand Prix the change over to turbocharged 1½-litre engines was almost complete. The life of the brilliant Ford-Cosworth V8 engine had finally come to an end with only three cars still faithful to the most successful racing engine ever built. Though a sad day in many ways, the change to turbocharging breathed life into what had been a stagnant development period for a number of years. We now saw seven different power packs available for Formula One

ENTRIES

DRIVER	TEAM	CAR
N. Piquet	Brabham	BMW 4-cyl t/c
C. Fabi	Brabham	BMW 4-cyl t/c
M. Brundle	Tyrrell	Tyrrell-Cosworth V8
S. Bellof	Tyrrell	Tyrrell-Cosworth V8
J. Laffite	Wiliams	FW09 Honda V6 t/c
K. Rosberg	Williams	FW09 Honda V6 t/c
A. Prost	McLaren	MP4/2Porsche V6 t/c
N. Lauda	McLaren	MP4/2 Porsche V6 t/c
P. Alliot	R.A.M.	R.A.M.-Hart 4 cyl t/c
J. Palmer	R.A.M.	R.A.M.-Hart 4-cyl t/c
E. de Angelis	Lotus	95T Renault V6 t/c
N. Mansell	Lotus	95T Renault V6 t/c
M. Winkelhock	A.T.S.	D7 B.M.W. 4-cyl t/c
P. Tambay	Renault	RE50 Renault V6 t/c
D. Warwick	Renault	RE50 Renault V6 t/c
M. Surer	Arrows	Arrows-Cosworth V8
T. Boutsen	Arrows	A7 B.M.W 4-cyl t/c
A. Senna	Toleman	TG184 Hart 4-cyl t/c
J. Cecotto	Toleman	TG184 Hart 4-cyl t/c
M. Baldi	Spirit	101/B Hart 4-cyl t/c
R. Patrese	Alfa Romeo	184T V8 t/c
E. Cheever	Alfa Romeo	184T V8 t/c
P. Ghinzani	Osella	Alfa Romeo V8 t/c
F. Hesnault	Ligier	Renault V6 t/c
A. de Cesaris	Ligier	Renault V6 t/c
M. Alboreto	Ferrari	126 C4 V6 t/c
R. Arnoux	Ferrari	126C4 V6 t/c
F. Serra	Arrows	Arrows-Cosworth V8

STARTING GRID

7
A. Prost
1 min. 22.66

12
N. Mansell
1 min. 22.75

28
R. Arnoux
1 min. 22.94

27
M. Alboreto
1 min. 22.94

16
D. Warwick
1 min. 23.24

15
P. Tambay
1 min. 23.41

26
A. de Cesaris
1 min. 23.58

8
N. Lauda
1 min. 23.89

1
N. Piquet
1 min. 23.92

6
K. Rosberg
1 min. 24.15

11
E. de Angelis
1 min. 24.43

14
M. Winkelhock
1 min. 24.47

19
A Senna
1 min. 25.01

22
R. Patrese
1 min. 25.10

2
C. Fabi
1 min. 25.29

5
J. Laffite
1 min. 25.72

25
F. Hesnault
1 min. 25.82

20
J. Cecotto
1 min. 25.87

24
P. Ghinzani
1 min. 25.88

4
S. Bellof
1 min. 26.12

use. The Brabham and Arrows teams were using the BMW M12/13 engine; Williams were Japanese powered with the Honda RA163-E; McLaren chose the TAG PO engine from Porsche; the Skoal Bandit team were powered by the Hart 415T, as were the Toleman and Spirit Racing team; the Benetton and the Osella teams had chosen the Alfa Romeo 183T engines; Ferrari, one of the pioneers with turbocharging, had their own 126C engine; Lotus and Ligier were using Renault EF4 engines, as of course were the other pioneer team - Renault. Only the Tyrrell team still used the latest DFY version of the Cosworth and some teams still had a spare Cosworth car tucked away in case their new motors wouldn't behave themselves on the day.

The Monaco organisers once again adapted the rules to suit themselves and all 27 entries were allowed to practice whereas 26 had been the limit for a number of previous races. This has never been popular with the drivers since overcrowding makes it difficult to achieve an unimpeded lap for the qualifying times. Nevertheless, as reference to the recorded times show, somehow most of them managed quite well, particularly the McLaren and Ferrari teams. Nigel Mansell in the Lotus had his share of problems, being well down the field after the Thursday session and having his practice car fail on the Saturday. He was forced to use his race car, which was being saved for the race, and put in a brilliant last minute effort which put him on the front row of the starting grid, next to Prost.

The only subject of conversation on race day was the weather. Whereas in 1983 the changeable conditions had made the race a tyre choice gamble, this time there were no doubts - it was wet weather tyres for everyone! Strangely enough in the downpour, a water tanker had to be sent to the tunnel to wet the road otherwise the sudden change from wet to dry and back to wet surface could have been dangerous.

Since the building of a new chicane at Ste. Devote a few years before, only one race had got underway without the corner gaining a first lap victim. This time Prost and Mansell were followed up the hill by Warwick and Arnoux side by side. Neither would give way and when the Ferrari bounced off the right hand kerb it side-swiped the Renault into the barrier on the left side of the road. Tambay in the second Renault was following closely and found his road blocked by his own team mate and the Renault team were both out of the race almost before it had begun. In the resulting chaos of

fast braking cars each taking avoiding action, de Cesaris, in another Renault powered car, collided with his team mate Hesnault and another car was out of the running.

The race, meanwhile, had settled down in the order: Prost (McLaren), Mansell (Lotus), Arnoux (Ferrari), Alboreto (Ferrari), Lauda (McLaren), Rosberg (Williams), Winkelhock (ATS), Lafitte (Williams), Senna (Toleman), Fabi (Brabham), Bellof (Tyrrell), Ghinzani (Osella), Piquet (Brabham), de Angelis (Lotus), Patrese (Alfa Romeo).

On lap seven Lauda passed both Alboreto and Arnoux on the same lap, to move into third place. The conditions were diabolical, with the road very slippery and the rain continuing to pour down. The spray thrown up by the wheels reduced visibility to only a few yards most

Bellof (Tyrrell) about to overtake Arnoux (Ferrari) for third place.

Inset
Mansell leads!

151

of the time and on lap 11 Prost came through the murk to the tunnel and found the road partially blocked by the Brabham of Fabi. As he carefully edged his way past, Mansell somehow found a way by and took the lead!

Mansell had frequently driven well at Monaco but this was the first time he had ever led the race. In the conditions Prost appeared to have no answer, and Nigel held his lead comfortably for six laps, increasing the margin steadily. Disaster was soon to follow however, again on the approach to Ste. Devote. The Lotus suddenly side slipped on painted road markings and struck the guard rail, damaging a rear wheel. He struggled on in an effort to get around to the pits but was unable to complete the lap.

In the conditions he was not the only one to make a mistake. Lauda in second place, spun in Casino Square and was forced to retire and there is no more experienced driver than Niki. Only the two newcomers Senna and Bellof seemed unaffected by the conditions. They were charging through the field together, rapidly cutting down Prost's lead, but the visibility was getting worse by the minute. The decision was made to end the race after 32 laps and the youngsters ran out of time leaving Prost the winner. Prost had possibly been lucky, with Mansell's disastrous error, and the abbreviated race, but nevertheless he had driven faultlessly in appalling conditions and not made the slightest error.

FORTY−SECOND

GRAND PRIX
OF MONACO
RESULTS

1st	A.Prost	McLaren TAG V6	lap 31	1 hr. 01 min. 07.74
2nd	A.Senna	Toleman Hart t/c 4	lap 31	1 hr. 1 min. 15.186
3rd	S.Bellof	Tyrrell Cosworth	lap 31	1 hrs. 1 min. 28.881
4th	R.Arnoux	Ferrari t/c V6	lap 31	1 hr. 1 min. 36.817
5th	K.Rosberg	Williams Honda V6	lap 31	1 hr. 1 min. 42.986
6th	E.de Angelis	Lotus Renault V6	lap 31	1 hr. 1 min. 52.179
7th	M.Alboreto	Ferrari t/c V6	lap 30	
8th	P.Ghinzani	Osella-Alfa Romeo	lap 30	
9th	J.Laffitte	Williams-Honda V6	lap 30	

Fastest lap: Ayrton Senna, lap 24, 1 min. 64.798 104.283 k.p.h.

Retired: R.Patrese *(Alfa Romeo V8)* lap 24, steering; N.Lauda *(McLaren TAG t/c V6)* lap 23, spun off; M.Winkelhock *(ATS-BMW t/c)* lap 22, spun off; N.Mansell *(Lotus Renault)* lap 15, hit barrier; N.Piquet *(Brabham BMW)* lap 14, electrics; F.Hesnault *(Ligier Renault)* lap 12, electrics; C.Fabi *(Brabham BMW)* lap 9, spun off; J.Cecotto *(Toleman-Hart)* lap 1, spun off; A.de Cesaris *(Ligier Renault)* lap 1, crash; D.Warwick *(Renault V6)* lap 0, crash; P.Tambay *(Renault V6)* lap 0, crash

Throughout the winter of 1984/85 there had been strong rumours that the sports governing body - F.I.S.A. were considering excluding the Monaco Grand Prix from the world championship. It has to be accepted that the old circuit is far from the ideal place to hold a motor race. Nevertheless the sport is dependent on commercial sponsorship and the money men like Monaco. They like its atmosphere, its social life, its glamour. Commercially it has a good image and that, at the end of the day proved to be more important than motor racing's technical objections.

So, once again, as May came around the complete circus was once again in attendance for the 43rd running

ENTRIES

DRIVER	TEAM	CAR
N. Lauda	McLaren	McLaren-Porsche V6 t/c
A. Prost	McLaren	McLaren-Porsche V6 t/c
M. Brundle	Tyrrell	Tyrrell-Cosworth V8
S. Bellof	Tyrrell	Tyrrell-Cosworth V8
N. Mansell	Williams	Williams-Honda V6 t/c
K. Rosberg	Williams	Williams-Honda V6 t/c
N. Piquet	Brabham	Brabham-B.M.W. t/c
F. Hesnault	Brabham	Brabham-B.M.W. t/c
M. Winkelhock	R.A.M.	R.A.M.-Hart 4 cyl t/c
P. Alliot	R.A.M.	R.A.M.-Hart 4 cyl t/c
E. de Angelis	Lotus	Lotus-Renault V6 t/c
A. Senna	Lotus	Lotus-Renault V6 t/c
P. Tambay	Renault	Renault-V6 t/c
D. Warwick	Renault	Renault-V6 t/c
G. Berger	Arrows	Arrows-B.M.W. 4 t/c
T. Boutson	Arrows	Arrows-B.M.W. 4 t/c
T. Fabi	Toleman	Toleman-Hart 4 t/c
R. Patrese	Alfa Romeo	Alfa Romeo V8 t/c
E. Cheever	Alfa Romeo	Alfa Romeo V8 t/c
P. Ghinzani	Osella	Osella-Alfa Romeo V8
A. de Cesaris	Ligier	Ligier-Renault V6 t/c
J. Laffite	Ligier	Ligier-Renault V6 t/c
M. Alboreto	Ferrari	Ferrari V6 t/c
S. Johansson	Ferrari	Ferrari V6 t/c
P. Martini	Minardi	Minardi-Moderni V6
J. Palmer	Zakspeed	Zakspeed 4 cyl t/c

STARTING GRID

12
A. Senna
1 min. 20.45

11
N. Mansell
1 min. 20.54

27
M. Alboreto
1 min. 20.56

23
E. Cheever
1 min. 20.73

2
A. Prost
1 min. 20.88

18
T. Boutsen
1 min. 21.30

6
K. Rosberg
1 min. 21.32

25
A. de Cesaris
1 min. 21.35

11
E. de Angelis
1 min. 21.47

16
D. Warwick
1 min. 21.53

17
G. Berger
1 min. 21.67

22
R. Patrese
1 min. 21.81

7
N. Piquet
1 min. 21.81

1
N. Lauda
1 min. 21.91

28
S. Johansson
1 min. 22.64

26
J. Laffite
1 min. 22.88

15
P. Tambay
1 min. 22.91

3
M. Brundle
1 min. 23.83

30
J. Palmer
1 min. 23.84

19
T. Fabi
1 min. 23.97

of the great race. There were 26 entries competing for the 20 starting grid places, headed by the Marlboro McLaren team of World Champion Niki Lauda and the '84 winner Alain Prost. The McLaren - powered by Porsche, was the ideal car for Monaco. It was tough enough mechanically to withstand rough treatment. It handled well, and most importantly it could out-accelerate any of its competitors from the slow bends.

The principal competition would come from the Williams-Hondas, driven by Mansell and Rosberg, and the Lotus-Renaults with Senna and de Angelis in the hot seats. Ayrton Senna, though still in only his second full season of Formula One, was once again star of the qualifying, leading the way on the Thursday with 1 min. 21.63. He improved this to 1 min. 20.45 on the Saturday and duly took the pole starting position.

Not that he had it all his own way, however. Nigel Mansell had had a number of creditable drives at Monaco, and a win was due soon. Alboreto in the Ferrari was another youngster not willing to hide his talents and Cheever made the best of the Alfa Romeo, though he appeared to be on the limit at times. All were conscious of the presence of Prost and Lauda though, who appeared to be happy with competent, if unspectacular, performances. At the other end of the scale, on their way home were Ghinzani (Osella), Bellof (Tyrrell), Alliot (Ram), Winkelhock(Ram), Hesnault (Brabham) and Martin (Minardi).

Tyre technology had developed to the stage that it was no longer enough to heat up a car's tyres on the warm up lap. In 1985 the teams used electrically heated tyre covers! But even the best of plans can go adrift. The blankets set Senna's tyres on fire entailing a frantic change of wheels minutes before the start!

Nevertheless he was still quickly away into the lead, even on cold tyres, followed by Mansell in the Williams. At the other end of the grid Berger, Tombay and Johansson had the shortest of races, colliding during the start. All three were too badly damaged to continue. Alboreto was very soon by Mansell and threatening Senna, but the leader was never easy to pass on any track, let alone the narrow streets of Monaco. In addition the Lotus was superior in power to the Ferrari and over the next seven laps a gap again opened up. However, the Renault engine let the leader down, blowing up on lap 10.

There are always many Ferrari fans at Monaco because of its close vicinity to Italy, and the sight of

Alboreto in the lead was greeted by enthusiastic cheering. Meanwhile Prost had moved up to second place when Mansell began to drop back. de Angelis was third, followed by Rosberg, Mansell, Warwick, Brundle and Boutsen.

Aboreto held his lead comfortably enough until lap 17 when he skidded on oil at Ste. Devote and took to the escape road. Although he only lost 15 seconds in getting going again, it was enough to allow Prost and his McLaren into the lead. Alboreto certainly hadn't given up though and it took him only a further six laps to catch and pass the leader.

Prost and the McLaren were not going as well as in practice, and though in second place he posed no real threat to the leader. The following order at half way was de Angelis (Lotus), de Cesaris (Ligier), Warwick (Renault), Laffite (Ligier), Rosberg and Mansell (Williams) together.

Above
Alboreto being chased by Prost. It took a puncture before the McLaren driver was able to gain the lead.

Top
The Lotus 97 driven by Elio de Angelis into third place.

155

Alain Prost entering Casino Square.

Soon after half way the leading Ferrari punctured a rear tyre and rushed into the pits for new rubber. It quickly rejoined the race, but now in fourth place. Prost now led from de Angelis and de Cesaris. Even so we still had not seen the last of Alboreto! The Ligier was little problem, but de Angelis in the Lotus was some way ahead and it took until lap 63 before he was able to regain second place. Time was now running out and though he cut down Prost's lead second by second, the chequered flag came for the McLaren before he could put in a real attack.

The laurel wreath went to Alain Prost but the honours were Alboreto's, for a truly memorable drive! Nevertheless - two wins in two years for Prost. Could he match Graham Hill's hat trick in 1986?

FORTY – THIRD
GRAND PRIX
OF MONACO
RESULTS

1st	A.Prost	McLaren MP4/28-5	lap 78	1 hr. 51 min. 58.034
2nd	M.Alboreto	Ferrari 156/85-081	lap 78	1 hr. 52 min. 05.575
3rd	E.de Angelis	Lotus 97T/1(T)	lap 78	1 hr. 53 min. 25.205
4th	A.de Cesaris	Ligier JS25/04	lap 77	
5th	D.Warwick	Renault RE60/03	lap 77	
6th	J.Laffite	Ligier JS25/01	lap 77	
7th	N.Mansell	Williams FW10/02	lap 77	
8th	K.Rosberg	Williams FW10/03	lap 76	
9th	T.Boutsen	Arrows A8/4	lap 76	
10th	M.Brundle	Tyrrell 012/6	lap 72	

Fastest lap: M.Alboreto (Ferrari 156/85-081), lap 60, 1 min. 22.637 144.284 k.p.h.

Retired: N.Lauda *(McLaren MP4/28-4)*lap 18, off track, stalled; R.Patrese *(Alfa Romeo 185T/2)*, lap 17, accident with Piquet; N.Piquet *(Brabham BT54/4)* lap 17, accident with Patrese; T.Fabi *(Toleman TG185/3)* lap lap 17, turbo failure A.Senna *(Lotus 97T/2)* lap 14, engine failure; E.Cheever *(Alfa Romeo 185T/3)* lap 11, electrical trouble; S.Johansson *(Ferrari 156/85-079)* lap 2, accident damage at start; G.Berger *(Arrows A8/3)* lap 1, accident at start; P.Tambay *(Renault RE60/02)(T)* lap 1, accident at start

There were two further alterations to the old Monaco circuit prior to the 1986 race. Both were in the interest of slowing the cars down and had been thought necessary with the Grand Prix cars becoming ever faster. The area from the tunnel exit, down the hill to the old chicane had been the scene of many accidents over the years. The chicane had been placed in various positions along the Quai Etats Unis without making very much difference because the cars were doing upwards of 170 m.p.h. down the hill onto the Quai. When the chicane was too close to the bottom of the hill the cars were braking hard while still coming down the hill. When the chicane was some way along the Quai, the cars

ENTRIES

DRIVER	TEAM	CAR
A. Prost	McLaren	McLaren-Porsche V6
K. Rosberg	McLaren	McLaren-Porsche V6
M. Brundle	Tyrrell	Tyrrell-Renault V6
P. Streiff	Tyrrell	Tyrrell-Renault V6
N. Mansell	Williams	Williams-Honda V6
N. Piquet	Williams	Williams Honda V6
R. Patrese	Brabham	Brabham-B.M.W.
E. de Angelis	Brabham	Brabham-B.M.W.
J. Dumfries	Lotus	Lotus-Renault V6
A. Senna	Lotus	Lotus-Renault V6
J. Palmer	Zakspeed	Zakspeed 4 cyl
A. Jones	Lola	Lola-Ford V6
P. Tambay	Lola	Lola-Ford V6
M. Surer	Arrows	Arrows-B.M.W.
T. Boutsen	Arrows	Arrows-B.M.W.
T. Fabi	Benetton	Benetton-B.M.W.
G. Berger	Benetton	Benetton-B.M.W.
P. Ghinzani	Osella	Osella-Alfa Romeo V8
C. Danner	Osella	Osella-Alfa Romeo V8
A. de Cesaris	Minardi	Minardi-Moderni V6
A. Nannini	Minardi	Minardi-Moderni V6
R. Arnoux	Ligier	Ligier-Renault V6
J. Laffite	Ligier	Ligier-Renault V6
M. Alboreto	Ferrari	Ferrari V6
S. Johansson	Ferrari	Ferrari V6
H. Rothengatter	Zakspeed	Zakspeed 4-cyl

STARTING GRID

1
A. Prost
1 min. 27.63

5
N. Mansell
1 min. 23.05

12
A. Senna
1 min. 23.18

27
M. Alboreto
1 min. 23.90

20
G. Berger
1 min. 23.96

7
R. Patrese
1 min. 24.12

26
J. Laffite
1 min. 24.40

16
P. Tambay
1 min. 24.69

2
K. Rosberg
1 min. 24.70

3
M. Brundle
1 min. 24.86

6
N. Piquet
1 min. 25.29

25
R. Arnoux
1 min. 25.54

4
P. Streiff
1 min. 25.72

18
T. Boutsen
1 min. 25.83

28
S. Johansson
1 min. 25.91

19
T. Fabi
1 min. 25.93

17
M. Surer
1 min. 26.30

15
A. Jones
1 min. 26.46

14
J. Palmer
1 min. 26.64

8
E. de Angelis
1 min. 27.19

Right
Clear view of the new chicane.

Top Right
**Brundle (Tyrrell), Tambay (Lola),
Piquet (Williams).**

Bottom Right
Nigel Mansell - Williams Honda V6.

approached it even faster. The new solution was to turn the chicane into a most definite slow left hand bend followed by a sweeping right hander onto the Quai. The other alteration which was definitely welcome was at the Rascasse Hairpin exit, in the area of the old Gasworks Harpin. Minor alterations had been made to the sweep into Boulevard Albert Premier making it safer yet faster.

There were 26 entries to fight over the 20 places on the grid. The two practice sessions were held on Thursday and Saturday this time, and were dominated by Alain Prost. The McLaren with its Porsche V6 engine, backed up by a very efficient team of mechanics, toured casually around until a suitable opportunity arose and then seemed to effortlessly put in the fastest lap. The new Ford engines - built by Cosworth - made an impressive first appearance in the Lolas, both qualifying well in the hands of Tambay and Jones. Clearly racing hasn't heard the last of the Cosworth name yet.

The Porsche engine was perfect for the Monaco circuit with tremendous acceleration out of the slow corners. With this advantage a driver of the stature of Prost looked unbeatable. The McLaren reputation for reliability was unrivalled in the Formula One series and with perfect dry sunny conditions, the betting man received very short odds on the World Champion. There were a number of cars on the grid with higher top speeds but this would not be of much use at Monaco. And so it was that Prost simply put the car into first gear and drove off to win the race, virtually unchallenged. It was not even a particularly fast race. Prost dominated from the front and when Rosberg, who had been in second place earlier

Kelemata
Data General
GOODYEAR
GOODYEAR
elf
3
VICTOR
VICTOR

Canon
Canon
Tactel
GOODYEAR
HONDA
Mobil 1
5
DENIM
calma
Canon
GOODYEAR
Canon
steinebronn

Alain Prost - World Champion and 1986 winner.

FORTY-FOURTH
GRAND PRIX
OF MONACO
RESULTS

in the race, reclaimed that place on lap 42, they were able to set their own pace, knowing they could answer any attempts to overtake with the sheer acceleration of their McLarens.

Senna in the Lotus held onto third place for most of the race, but was unable to put in a serious challenge to the leaders. Likewise Mansell. This year the Williams was just not at its best for Monaco.

So it has to be admitted that there is little more to tell. Complete domination leads to a dull race, but fortunately there have been very few years in which such superiority was so apparent.

1st	A.Prost	McLaren-Porsche	lap 78	1 hr. 55 min. 41.060
2nd	K.Rosberg	McLaren-Porsche	lap 78	1 hr. 56 min. 06.082
3rd	A.Senna	Lotus 98T-Renault	lap 78	1 hr. 56 min. 34.706
4th	N.Mansell	William-Honda V6	lap 78	1 hr. 56 min. 52.462
5th	R.Arnoux	Ligier JS27-Renault	lap 77	
6th	J.Laffite	Ligier JS27-Renault	lap 77	
7th	N.Piquet	Williams-Honda V6	lap 77	
8th	T.Boutsen	Arrows A8-BMW	lap 75	
9th	M.Surer	Arrows A8-BMW	lap 75	
10th	S.Johansson	Ferrari F1/86-V6	lap 75	
11th	P.Streiff	Tyrrell 015-Renault	lap 74	
12th	J.Palmer	ZAK 861-Zakspeed	lap 74	

Fastest Lap: A.Prost (McLaren MP4/2C) lap 51, 1 min. 26.607 136.80 k.p.h.

Retired: M.Brundle *(Tyrrell 015/Renault V6)* lap 68, retired; P.Tambay *(Lola THL2/86-Ford V6)*, lap 68, retired; G. Berger *(Benetton B186-BMW 4 cyl)* lap 43, retired; M.Alboreto *(Ferrari F1/86-Ferrari V6)* lap 39, retired; R.Patrese *(Brabham BT55-BMW 4 cyl)* lap 39, retired; E.de Angelis *(Brabham BT55-BMW 4 cyl)* lap 32, retired; T.Fabi *(Benetton B186-BMW 4 cyl)* lap 18, retired; A.Jones *(Lola THL 2/86-Ford V6)*, lap 3, retired.